Pathways of America
The California Gold Rush Trail

by
Lynda Hatch

illustrated by Kathryn R. Marlin

Cover by Kathryn R. Marlin

Copyright © 1994, Good Apple

ISBN No. 0-86653-810-0

Printing No. 987654

Good Apple
A Division of Frank Schaffer Publications, Inc.
23740 Hawthorne Boulevard
Torrance, CA 90505-5927

Table of Contents

GA1502

Dedication

To my friends at The High Desert Museum in Bend, Oregon, who
explored parts of the California Trail with me . . .

And to our family pioneers who traveled the trail . . .
the Oldfield family that traveled from England to Utah, and then to
California in 1864

the Bennett family that left Wisconsin, crossed the Isthmus of
Panama, and took a ship to California in 1855

GA1502

Introduction

Pathways of America: The California Gold Rush Trail covers the cross-country journey the emigrants and Forty-Niners faced as they traveled from the Missouri River to the Sacramento Valley and mining camps in California. Each of the major sites is highlighted in the order in which it would have been encountered on the trip. Alternate routes near the Great Salt Lake, over the Sierra Nevada Mountains, and across the oceans are also described. Information and activities about life in California once the emigrants arrived are also included. The California Trail followed the Oregon Trail until past Fort Bridger, and then several trail routes were available, depending on the year. For this reason, the book concentrates on the routes and locations past Fort Bridger. For general information, activities, and more detail on the beginning of the route, see *Pathways of America: The Oregon Trail.*

The book includes detailed background information, emigrant journal quotations, stories that will be remembered by the students, and a bibliography. Quality activities for the students accompany each site and route to teach about life on the trail, natural and cultural information, geography and science concepts, integration of language arts and math skills, and information about historic sites. The activities are purposely designed in an open-ended manner, with few right and wrong answers, to allow students of all ages and abilities to ponder and tackle the problems.

The information is detailed to provide the teacher with a thorough, accurate background on the journey. Teachers usually don't have access to all the books that contain the amount of detail that is needed for their teaching. Hopefully this book will provide that resource for the teacher. Although it is detailed, it will also be of interest to students, whether they read it on their own or they hear the stories read aloud to them. The book attempts to cover the information accurately. As with any history, there are often differing opinions, so numerous sources were used to get the most accepted information. Notice that when journals are quoted, the spelling and punctuation are left in their original forms.

As they study the California Trail using the resources provided in this guide, your students will become fascinated by these amazing journeys, and they might even be inspired to seek adventures of their own, to enrich their own lives, and contribute knowledge and understanding for all people.

Note: The term *Indian* has been used here as it was during pioneer days. Today, some people prefer the term *Indian*, some prefer *Native American*, and some feel either is fine. So as not to offend anyone, it is important to use the term that is most preferred in your area.

GA1502

Before You Begin

If the definitions for the following words are clear, the concepts in this book will be easier. Reading history can be difficult because of words that aren't in use today. Students will enjoy the spellings and word usages of the pioneer journal quotations. The text in this guide is written as background information for the teacher and for the students. Depending on individual abilities, teachers may need to guide students through the reading.

alkali
Argonaut
ascent/descent
Bear Flag Revolt
blacksmith
bonanza
British/English/England
carbonated water
carbon dioxide
carcass
carrion
cathedral/steeple
Catholic missions
chlorophyll/pigment
cholera
chromatography
Compromise of 1850
condensation/water cycle
contamination
cradle (rocker)
culture clash
Diggers
economic depression
emigrant/immigrant
encephalitis
elevation
epidemic
eureka
expedition
fording (a stream)
Forty-Niner

fur trade
geology
gold rush
guidebook
granite
hard rock mine
Hudson's Bay Company
hydraulic mining
indigenous
isthmus
journal
land grant
landlocked basin
lava flow/volcanic
lice
Long Tom
lye
malaria
Manifest Destiny
Mexican War
mining strike
mirage
Mohs' scale
monotonous
Mormons
Mother Lode
mulatto
naturalist
oasis
ore
Oregon Trail

panorama
photosynthesis
placer mining
Pony Express
prejudice
prospector
pyramid
rain shadow effect
reservoir
sagebrush
scurvy
"seeing the elephant"
Sierra Nevada Mountains
sluice
soda springs
stake a claim
sulphur
tail race
teamster
telegraph
ticket scalper
tragedy
Treaty of Guadalupe Hidalgo
Transcontinental Railroad
U.S. Mint
vein (in rock)
voyage
wagon train
water-powered sawmill
yellow fever

Note: *Pioneer*, borrowed from the French *pionnier*, is a derivation of the Old French *paonier*. The form originally denoted a foot soldier sent ahead to clear the way. This was a derivation of *paon*, a foot soldier. Today, *pioneer* means "a person or group that explores new areas of thought or activity." Pioneers begin or take part in the development of something new and go first to prepare the way for others.

GA1502

Map of the California Trail

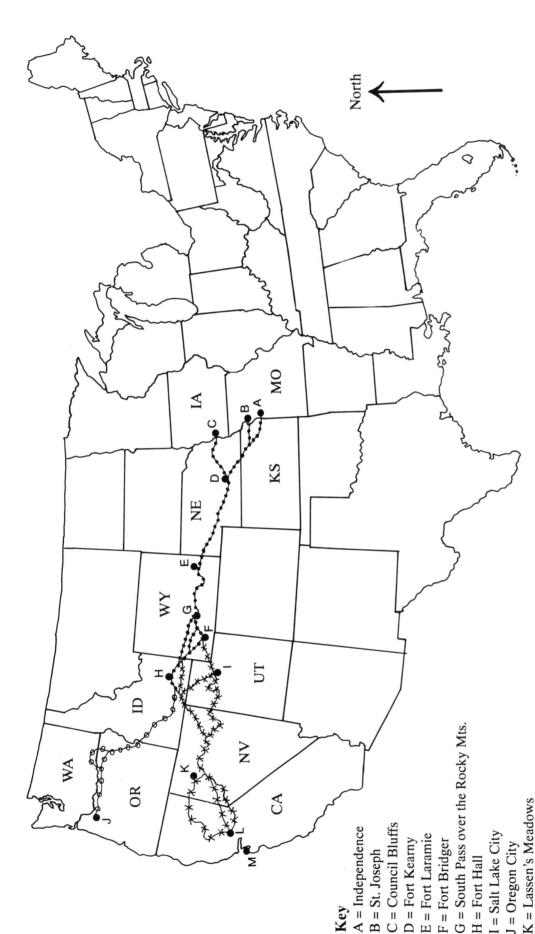

Until the Fort Bridger area, the California Trail and the Oregon Trail followed the same route (and a few alternative routes). In the Fort Bridger/South Pass area, there were several alternative routes for the California Trail. The trail came back together as one main route along the Humboldt River. The California Trail again split into alternative routes as it crossed the Sierra Nevada Mountains until it finally reached the Sacramento Valley. Alternative routes developed over different years so they were not available as choices every year of the emigration.

Key
A = Independence
B = St. Joseph
C = Council Bluffs
D = Fort Kearny
E = Fort Laramie
F = Fort Bridger
G = South Pass over the Rocky Mts.
H = Fort Hall
I = Salt Lake City
J = Oregon City
K = Lassen's Meadows
L = Sacramento (Sutter's Fort)
M = San Francisco

Routes
•—•—• Route of the combined California and Oregon Trails
o—o—o Route of the Oregon Trail
x—x—x Route of the California Trail

Background Information on the California Trail

The journey along the California Trail was long, difficult, and often monotonous. The first part across the prairies followed the Oregon Trail and was the easiest. There were several alternate routes over the years, but they all included mountains, then deserts, and then more mountains before they reached the Sacramento Valley in California. There were many miles of intense heat, a lack of water, and too much sand. The emigrants who traveled late in the season often struggled through mountain snows. Their enemy was "distance against time." They had to travel 2000 miles (3220 km) and had to do it within the limits of one summer and fall. There were breakdowns of the wagons, and equipment was sometimes lost by accident. When the wagons became too heavy for the oxen to pull, supplies and equipment had to be thrown out along the trail. Even though there were a few emigrant guides, the people were generally ignorant of what conditions would be like. This ignorance and their general optimism made it possible for them to succeed. When one man learned what life on the trail was really like, he said that if he could ever get back to Missouri, he would gladly eat out of the trough with his hogs!

The emigrants dealt with their hardships and took one step at a time toward California. Elisha Perkins wrote (1849): "Now we were out of civilization & the influences of civilized society entirely, & cut loose from the rest of the world to take care of ourselves for a while. I confess to a feeling of lonliness as I thought on the prospects before us, & all we were separating ourselves from behind. Henceforth we shall have no society, no sympathy in our troubles & none of the comforts to which we have been accustomed, but must work across these vast wild wastes alone & go in our own strength & his who takes care of us all. So be it. Gold must be had & I for one am willing to brave most anything in its acquisition." (Rather than gold, he found death in his early twenties in 1852.)

The first routes that were followed to California were trails of the Indians, fur traders, and even game trails. The routes were dictated by geography as well as available resources such as water, game, firewood, and forage for livestock.

3

GA1502

Reasons for Emigrating to California

There were many reasons pioneers set out across the plains or seas to go to California. Some were reasons that made them want to leave where they were (pushed them out) and other reasons made them want to be in California (pulled them West).

One reason to leave the Mississippi Valley, where many emigrants came from, was because of disease. Much of the land was undrained and swampy, so malaria was common. John Bidwell, one of the first California pioneers, remembered a meeting of prospective emigrants where John Roubideaux, an early promoter of California, tried to convince people that there was a healthy climate. Bidwell wrote: "Generally the first question which a Missourian asked about a country was whether there was fever or ague [malaria]. I remember his answer distinctly. He said there was but one man in California that has ever had a chill [from malaria] there, and it was a matter of so much wonderment to the people of Monterey that they went 18 miles into the country to see him shake. Nothing could have been more satisfactory on the score of health . . . ." There were always rumors like these associated with moving to California.

Taxes were high in the Mississippi Valley because of many canals that were built and had to be paid for by the public. By the late 1830s the United States was in the worst economic depression it had been in in all of its history. It was hard for farmers to sell their crops. Also, more and more people had moved to these former frontier lands and people now felt crowded and wanted to move on. Many had already moved once, and some more often, so to move again was only natural. For some people, leaving was an escape from debts and the law. They could start their lives over.

Other people felt drawn to California. Some were restless or bored and were seeking adventure and a better life. They wanted their own land in a good climate. For some Catholics there was the pull of going to a land where their own faith was the established church. There was the possibility of a good, solid religious education for their children at the missions. After the discovery of gold in California in 1848, many Forty-Niners headed West to seek their fortunes. The people who journeyed West in the early years and again after the gold fever ended were basically family units that had been able to put together enough money for this type of journey. They were farmers, merchants, and professional people who saw new opportunities to be in on the start of something new. Unlike the Forty-Niners, many of whom were single men who hoped to strike it rich and return to the U.S., these people were going West with the idea of building a new life for themselves and their children.

GA1502

The pioneers going West were called emigrants because until about 1847, they were leaving the United States. Mexico owned California and Utah, and the British still held Oregon. Some emigrants probably did not care that they were actually leaving the United States behind. Others felt that in some small way, they were part of a larger historic event and felt it was their duty to move West to help expand the country. They often painted patriotic slogans on their wagon covers. In 1845 the idea of "Manifest Destiny" was the belief that the U.S. had a God-given right to own, settle, and develop the rest of the country. It was not a national "program" to help emigrants move West, and the government did not build the trail. However, the government was aware that having U.S. citizens move to these new lands might eventually help the U.S. claim them as American lands. The emigrants were actually on their own. The movement was a spontaneous, grass-roots event in American life. When they moved West, they carried with them the ideals of law and social order, the customs, the religious traditions, and the political and economic forms of government of the U.S.

Reuben Shaw wrote his reasons as to why people emigrated (1849): "The mystery attached to the country which we were to traverse, the novelty of the undertaking, the prospect of lively adventure and in some cases, the benefits that were expected to be derived from a change from the counting-room to life in the open air seemed to be the primary incentives to their crossing the plains." Another man wrote: ". . . to see something of Indian life, and indulge in hunting on the plains, and all that sort of thing." James Clyman, a mountain man, wrote how the emigration puzzled him (1846): "It is strange that so many of all kinds and classes of People should sell out comfortable homes in Missouri and Elsewhere pack up and start across such an emmence Barren waste to settle in some new place of which they have at most so uncertain information. But this is the character of my countrymen." He also said: ". . . the human mind can never be satisfied never at rest allways on the strech for something new some strange novelty."

GA1502

Graphing the Number of Emigrants to California Activity
Reasons for Emigrating to California

The following statistics show the approximate number of emigrants that went to California by the overland route between 1841 and 1860.

Make a line graph *or* bar graph to show this data.

1841	34	1851	1100
1842	0	1852	50,000
1843	38	1853	20,000
1844	53	1854	12,000
1845	260	1855	1500
1846	1500	1856	8000
1847	450	1857	4000
1848	400	1858	6000
1849	25,000	1859	17,000
1850	44,000	1860	9000

After you have made your graph, study the data. Write down some questions you would like to have answered, based on the data you see. Research the answers to these questions. For example, when looking at the data, you might see the results of the discovery of gold at Sutter's Creek, the Donner Party tragedy, and the war with Mexico.

Example:
Question: In 1842, no emigrants left the United States for California. However, was anything new learned about the trail that year that would help future emigrants?

Answer: Yes–Joseph Chiles, who had gone to California in 1841 as a member of the Bartleson Party, made a return trip East in 1842. Chiles' group followed the route "backwards" as far as the Green River (and then swung south to New Mexico and on to Missouri, avoiding Sioux warbands) so they more thoroughly learned part of the route.

GA1502

Beginning of the Trail–
Death from Cholera at Red Vermillion Crossing

Until the emigrants reached western Wyoming, the California Trail and the Oregon Trail followed the same route. Along this route in northeast Kansas, Red Vermillion Crossing was a popular emigrant campsite with wood, grass, and water. The area was also a site of great tragedy. In May of 1849, a large group of emigrants camped here. Many became sick and died with Asiatic cholera, a dreaded disease. At least fifty people are believed to be buried on the east riverbank. This burial site is now a National Historic Site called the Oregon Trail Cholera Cemetery. It is also referred to as the "49'ers Cemetery." Today, three limestone grave markers can be seen inside a chain link fence. Only one has chiseled letters: "T.S. Prather, May 27, 1849."

Forty-Niner David Dewolf wrote of the first graves on the Red Vermillion riverbank: "May 31, 1849. We next crossed the little Vermillion which has very steep banks and rapid current. On the bank of this stream were 6 graves all died with colery . . . ." Kimball Wester who traveled later in 1849 saw many new graves along the trail and wrote: "That very much dreaded scourge, the Asiatic cholera, is making such sad havoc among the Californias that almost every campground is converted into a burial ground."

Cholera was spread by contaminated water. In those days, little was known about sanitation or how diseases were spread. When a person became sick or had an accident, he or she only had about three choices: opiates, amputation, and prayer. Cholera struck hard and fast, causing diarrhea, vomiting, fever, chills, cramps, convulsions, and often death. People in cities died from cholera at about the same rate as people on the trail. Even President Zachary Taylor died of cholera in 1850. People could be fine in the morning, have agonizing stomach pains by noon, and be dead by evening.

Since emigrants usually had no lumber for coffins, they wrapped the bodies in cloth and buried them under rocks and packed earth. Some graves were dug in the ruts of the wagon trail, in hopes that Indians or wolves would not be able to find them and dig up the bodies. Emigrant Agnes Stewart saw a piece of woman's hair sticking out of the trail with a comb still in it and wrote that she "would as soon not be buried at all as to be dug out of my own grave."

In addition to diseases being spread by emigrants who didn't know about sanitation, they didn't treat the land carefully because, selfishly, they felt they would never go back to those sites. Another wagon train would come to the campsite the next day and camp in the same filth. Opportunities for bathing and laundering were limited. Human and animal waste, garbage, animal carcasses, and water supplies were often close together. In many areas, pure drinking water was not available.

 GA1502

Growing Microbes on Potato Slices Activity
Death from Cholera at Red Vermillion Crossing, Kansas

To learn more about disease microbes (germs), they can be grown in a safe way. Have an adult help with these steps:

1. Cut a raw potato into thick slices, each about $\frac{1}{4}$" (.6 cm) thick.

2. Boil these potato slices until they are hot and softer than when raw, but not mushy. Let them cool slightly so they are warm, but still moist, so the germs will grow well.

3. Decide how many potato slices to use. Get that many plastic sandwich bags that zip shut. Place about 4" (10 cm) of masking tape near the opening of the plastic bag. On the tape, write your name, the date, and what will be done to each potato, to see what germs will grow there. Examples:
   - Rub fingers over the potato slice
   - Breathe on the surface of the potato
   - Expose a potato slice to the air for an hour
   - Sneeze on the potato slice
   - Spit on the potato slice
   - Place dog or cat's saliva on a potato slice

Note: As long as blood is not used, dangerous disease germs will not be created. Throw the bag and potato away when the experiment is over.

4. Place the potato slice on a small square of tagboard or cardboard. Place three toothpicks straight up on each potato slice after the germs have been added. Slip one potato slice into each bag and zip each shut. The toothpicks will hold the bag up like a tent so the plastic won't smash the "germ garden" as it grows.

5. Each day, watch for the growth of clumps of microbes. If clumps are growing, they will usually appear as big spots (often orange), gray fuzz, or as a white web. Through research, the types of microbes could be determined. Look at these microbes under a microscope or a hand lens. Each day, draw, color, and write a description of the microbe clumps, noting the differences from the day before.

GA1502

Map of Trail Choices Just West of Fort Bridger

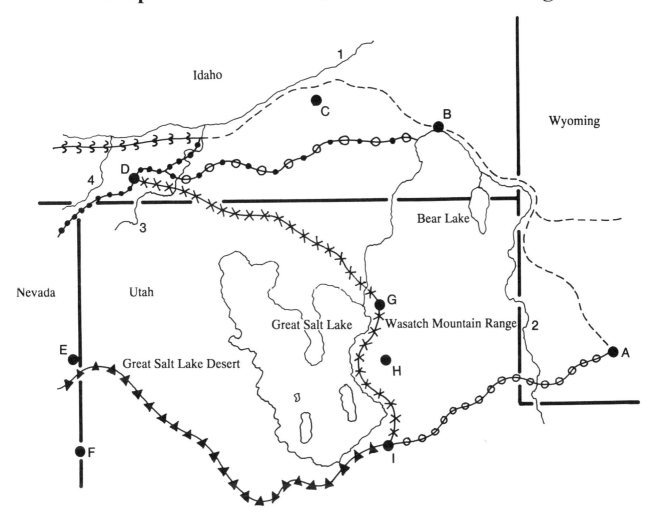

Key

Routes

o o o o — Mormon-Salt Lake Route (Donner Party, 1846)

• o • o • Hudspeth Cutoff

✕ ✕ ✕ ✕ Salt Lake Trail

• • • • • Fort Hall-Raft River Route

▲ ▲ ▲ ▲ Hastings Cutoff (Donner Party, 1846)

– – – – Combined California and Oregon Trails

ᛤ ᛤ ᛤ ᛤ Oregon Trail

A = Fort Bridger
B = Soda Springs
C = Pocatello (Fort Hall)
D = Silent City of Rocks
E = Pilot Peak
F = Wendover
G = Brigham City
H = Ogden
I = Salt Lake City

1 = Snake River
2 = Bear River
3 = Raft River
4 = Goose Creek

North

9

Decision at Fort Hall

About fifty miles west of Fort Hall, at the Raft River, the trail to California branched off from the Oregon Trail. British fur traders from the Hudson's Bay Company ran Fort Hall. They encouraged the emigrants to choose the California route. At that time, it hadn't been decided whether England or the United States would own the Oregon Country. The British figured that the more Americans they could convince to move south to California, the better their chances were at eventually owning Oregon.

People who had already settled in California were also eager for more Americans to choose California. Sometimes they even went to Fort Hall to try to persuade them to come. For example, in 1845, Caleb Greenwood and his sons went by horseback to Fort Hall to meet the emigrants going west. He was a very effective speaker and talked to the emigrants about the advantages of going to California instead of Oregon. Greenwood did this partly for his own benefit and also to help Captain Johann Augustus Sutter who had a fort in the Sacramento Valley of California. Sutter had a large land grant and wanted people to live on his land. Greenwood tried to convince emigrants to settle on Sutter's land. He also planned to hire himself out as a guide and collect $2.50 for each wagon he led.

Jarvis and Truman Bonney, brothers from Illinois, and their families were at Fort Hall when Greenwood was there. Seven-year-old Benjamin, one of the Bonney children, later remembered what happened. "Greenwood . . . was dressed in buckskins and had a long heavy beard and used very picturesque language. He called the Oregon emigrants together the first evening we were in Fort Hall and made a talk. He said the road to Oregon was dangerous on account of the Indians . . . to California there was an easy grade and crossing the mountains would not be difficult . . . Sutter would supply them with plenty of potatoes, coffee, and dried beef. He also said he would help the emigrants over the mountains with their wagons and that to every head of a family who would settle near Sutter's Fort, Captain Sutter would give six sections of land of his Spanish grant land." Greenwood had exaggerated, but it had caused the emigrants to consider changing to the California route.

Benjamin described what happened then. "Next morning old Caleb Greenwood . . . said that all you who want to go to California . . . follow me." He repeated why California was better. From this wagon train, eight wagons decided to go to California. Benjamin remembered that as the Oregon emigrants continued on, they shouted back, "Good-bye, we will never see you again. Your bones will whiten in the desert or be gnawed by the wild animals in the mountains."

GA1502

Publicizing the Advantages of Your State Activity
Decision at Fort Hall

Caleb Greenwood went to Fort Hall to convince Oregon Trail emigrants to change to the California Trail. He was quite successful because he was a good speaker. Even though he exaggerated, he used logical arguments to try to convince the emigrants. For example, Benjamin Bonney remembered Greenwood saying, ". . . You will find there are no Indians to kill you, the roads are better, and you will be allowed to take up more land in California than in Oregon, and the climate is better. There is plenty of hunting and fishing and the rivers are full of salmon." He knew just what to say to convince people. Jarvis Bonney was a fisherman, and one of his main reasons for going West was because he heard great stories of trout and salmon in the rivers. Jarvis' wagon was the first one to decide to go to California instead of Oregon. Altogether Greenwood convinced fifty wagons to change to California. He earned $125 to be their guide, which was excellent pay in those days.

Imagine that you work for your state's Visitors Bureau. Like Caleb Greenwood, your job is to convince people to move to your state. Decide what you would say to convince them to come.

1. Make a chart and divide it into two parts. As a title of one part write "Reasons to move to my state." (Before you can win an argument, it is always important to know the "bad" side–what people will say against your argument. In that way, you can be prepared to "counter" their argument.)

2. Fill out both sides of the chart, listing as many specific reasons as you can. For example, a good reason might be because there are beautiful places for people to camp in the mountains. A bad reason might be that there are not many jobs for people.

3. Look carefully at the "Reasons to move to my state" side. Combining as many of these reasons as you can, draw and color a poster that the Visitors Bureau might use in its advertising to try to get people to move to your state. Be sure to put a title on your poster and, like all artists, sign your artwork with your name.

4. You might really take your poster to your state's Visitors Bureau and show them. They will be pleased that you are so proud of your state. Who knows, they might actually want to use it! When you are at the Visitors Bureau, look at the brochures that have been printed about your state. See if the advantages they list for your state are the same ones you chose.

5. This project could also be done about your city or county.

GA1502

Oregon-California Trail Junction to City of Rocks
Yale, Idaho, to Almo, Idaho

The emigrants who chose the California Trail west of Fort Hall followed the level, barren plain along the Raft River. The valley was surrounded by high hills often covered with black rocks. Grass could usually be found along the river bottom. The tops of the hills, however, had little vegetation except for a few fir trees and cedar trees. This section of the trail was not particularly hard travel, although it was dusty in some spots. J. Goldsborough Bruff wrote (1849): "The fresh breeze nearly suffocated us with clouds of blinding, stifling dust–right in our faces. We camped on the bank of the stream . . . Such beards and faces!–all white with dust–our animals ditto. A wash was quite refreshing."

There were very few days when they didn't have to travel. Wakeman Bryarly appreciated one July morning along the Raft River when they got to relax. He wrote (1849): "This morning we were astonished at not hearing our usual summons 'To horse,' and lay for some time basking in the sunshine of a bright, fresh, clear and glorious morning, wondering what could be the cause of such unusual thing as being allowed to let the sun catch us in our blankets . . . we were to spend this delightful morning in camp. Thank God we had no mosquitoes last night, and we arose fully refreshed . . . The men amused themselves in fishing, bathing, and washing their clothes."

Even though it was tempting to linger along the route, the emigrants knew that they must keep on their journey or they might become stuck in the mountains by winter snows. As the summer came to an end, they noticed that the nights were getting colder. Bruff wrote (1849): "Patches of snow on the adjacent mountains. We were all white this morning on awakening, with frost, and my hair being very long, the ends were froze to the saddle (pillow) and ground, so that I had to pull it loose, but had to leave some, as a momento for the wolves to examine,–I thought of the picture in Gulliver's travels, where the Liliputians had picketed his hair down while he slept."

GA1502

Recording Beautiful Scenes Activity
Oregon-California Trail Junction to City of Rocks

The emigrants could rarely take time to relax and enjoy the scenery, but when they could, the time was appreciated. James Pritchard wrote about the valley of the Raft River (1849): "beautifully surrounded by high mountains the taller peaks of which are covered with perpetual snows . . . we found plenty of good grass, wood and water . . . About sunset I found my way to the top of one of the nearest peaks, from the top of which I had a most spacious view of the surrounding country. The south side of this peak was covered with seeder [cedar] and grass, and the top with shivered stone and the north with snow—and the whole with mosquitoes."

The emigrants were often thrilled with the sights they saw and recorded the details in their journals. Elisha Perkins was amazed at what was found along the trail and wrote (1849): ". . . passed by the road side near our camp a bed of real Wethersfield onions . . . They probably are the products of some seed thrown out as spoiled by some settler, or they may be indigenous. I have repeatedly picked and eaten wild garlic of fine flavor. Heard the short sweet notes of a solitary brown thrush . . . His notes resembled exactly our brown thrush and like everything I see which is rare here [brings] recollections of the pleasant home and dear friends I have left behind me . . . Even the bed of old fashioned onions nearly made the tears come. They looked so like old acquaintances!"

Even though they were tired, the emigrants often took the time to sketch or write descriptions of the beautiful and unusual sights they saw along the trail. They wanted to remember what they had seen and hopefully someday to share these memories with their friends and relatives in the East who had not made the journey. You can record a beautiful or unusual place in your state, as well.

1. Choose a place in your state that you think is very beautiful or very unusual. Either visit the place or look at many pictures of it so you feel you "know it" well.

2. Through sketching, painting, photography, and/or very descriptive writing, record the details of your special place. Think of all the senses—seeing, hearing, smelling, tasting, touching—and see how many of them you can include in your details. Be sure to tell the name and location of the place.

3. Share your writing or art with someone else so he or she can learn about your special place too.

Salt Lake Trail
Salt Lake City, Utah, to Silent City of Rocks, Idaho

Beyond South Pass, the trail divided into several routes. The emigrants had to make a choice as to which way was best for them. Those who were in the worst need of new equipment followed the Mormon Road to Salt Lake City. They could perhaps trade some of their dry food such as beans and rice for fresh vegetables and some exhausted oxen for fresh ones. This shortened the route that in earlier years would have led them north to Fort Hall.

In 1848 Captain Samuel Hensley developed a shortcut to California which went north of the Great Salt Lake, across Bear River, to the Silent City of Rocks. At first he thought the best route for packers was across the Hastings Cutoff to the east of Salt Lake City. However, his group was caught in a violent summer cloudburst on the salt flats. The water softened the salt crust on the soil, turning it into mud and mush. The animals bogged down immediately. Equipment and food had to be thrown out in order to save the animals. The emigrants struggled for forty-eight hours without food or fresh water. Finally they were able to retrace their path and return to Salt Lake City to get more supplies. They were not in a mood to try Hastings Cutoff again. The road to Fort Hall was the safest route, but it was discouragingly long. Hensley and his men decided to try a new route. They went north about eighty miles and then forded the Bear River. They boldly set out across unknown land to the northwest. Eventually, after a three- to four-day ride, they came through a gap between the mountains and recognized Cathedral Spires (also known as Cathedral Towers and Twin Sisters), the southern part of the Silent City of Rocks. They had rejoined the main trail.

A few weeks later, members of the Mormon Battalion were traveling east from California to Salt Lake City after having just opened Carson Pass over the Sierra Mountains. After talking to the wagon trains they passed going west, they were confused as to the best route to Salt Lake City. Along the trail they also met Hensley and were interested in his new route. When they reached Cathedral Spires, they knew that was the right spot to leave the Raft River and follow Hensley's route southeast to Salt Lake City. These returning Mormons were the first to take wagons over this new Salt Lake Trail.

GA1502

Creating a Mushy, Mucky, Muddy Desert Floor Activity
Salt Lake Trail

Captain Samuel Hensley and his packers developed the Salt Lake Trail in 1848 after getting stuck on the Hastings Cutoff and needing a new route. They became completely bogged down when they were caught in a violent summer storm east of Salt Lake City. The desert floor turned to mud, muck, and mush. Wagons and animals became stuck, and it took two days for Hensley and his men to dig out and return to Salt Lake City for new supplies.

You can create a substance that reacts like the desert ground during a cloudburst. A mixture of cornstarch and water can show the characteristics of liquids and solids and create a surface of "muck."

1. Mix $1/4$ cup water with green and red food coloring. This mixture should create a light-brown color (about 15-20 drops) to look like the desert ground. Mix this in a bucket or other large container.

2. Slowly add small amounts of cornstarch to the water and mix it with a very strong spoon or swirl it in the bucket. Keep adding small amounts of cornstarch until the mixture is able to *flow* but will *feel hard* when you *press* it. This will take about $1/2$ cup of cornstarch.

3. Cover your work area with newspaper. Have damp paper towels handy for wiping your hands. Scoop the mixture into a pie tin.

4. Investigate the mixture to learn about its properties. When does it behave like a solid? When does it behave like a liquid? How does it behave when you press on it? What other properties does it have? Test your ideas by experimenting.

GA1502

5. Emigrant wagons and cattle got stuck in the muck of the wet desert floor, which was similar to this cornstarch mixture. Try designing a new type of wagon that the emigrants could have used for traveling west, but that would not have gotten stuck in the desert mud. Using all the "junk" you can find, your engineering skills, and your creativity, build a model of a new wagon. For example, you might start with an aluminum soda can and add attachments so it looks like a wagon and is adapted for traveling in mud. Then gently push the wagon into your cornstarch mixture. Try to lift the wagon out with just your two little fingers. Were you successful, or did your wagon become stuck? If it stuck, what modifications could you make so it wouldn't get stuck the next time? When you feel you have succeeded, display your new model. Label it with a clever name and include a written description of how this new wagon would work, why it would work, and why it would not get stuck in the mud. Instead of a three-dimensional model, this design could also be done in a drawing (without the testing in the cornstarch mixture, of course).

6. The cornstarch mixture can be saved for another day by putting it in the refrigerator. It can also be dried out overnight and then more water added the next day. Do not pour the mixture into the sink as it is likely to clog the drain. If a large amount spills, scoop up most of it. Then wipe up the remaining mixture with a sponge.

GA1502

Hudspeth Cutoff
Soda Springs to Cassia Creek at the Raft River, Idaho

On July 19, 1849, Benoni Hudspeth and John Myers led their wagon train off the main trail along the Bear River, starting a new cutoff to California. At Soda Springs they headed west, hoping to save miles and time by avoiding the loop north to Fort Hall. Also, if they could get away from the crowds on the main trail, they would be able to find better grass for their cattle.

In 1841 the Bidwell-Bartleson wagon train had headed to California in this general direction, but a bit to the south. Therefore, the Hudspeth train had to establish their own trail. Myers went out ahead as a guide, searching for a route. Hudspeth, the captain, followed with the other emigrants and wagons. They broke trail across volcanic, sagebrush-covered plains. At one wide crack in the ground, left from an ancient lava flow, they rolled big rocks in, piled brush and earth on top, and took the wagons over. Myers generally knew which direction to travel but didn't know if he was leading the wagons over a route that would be impossible. The area contained many mountain ranges that ran north and south. They were difficult to cross and it was a long journey to go around them. Myers was lucky. He found a way through the mountains with enough grass and water to get them through alive. What he didn't realize was that many of the other wagons on the main trail had seen the tracks of the Hudspeth wagons. They had assumed that was the proper way to go and had followed. It would have been very confusing if Myers had not found a route, and they all would have had to return to the trail to Fort Hall.

They hoped the cutoff would come out along the Humboldt River. However, on July 24 they arrived at the Raft River Trail that had led southwest from Fort Hall, miles before the Humboldt. They ended up among the wagons they had traveled with earlier, almost in the same position in line. The cutoff had avoided the big loop to Fort Hall but had to follow many smaller loops and twists to get through the mountains. They had saved little time, but since they were breaking trail, future emigrants that would follow the cutoff would be able to travel a little faster. Even though it was debatable whether it saved time or miles, from then on most California emigrants used this cutoff. The route through Fort Hall and along the Raft River was used by fewer and fewer California emigrants. This new route was usually named the Hudspeth Cutoff but was also known as the Myers Cutoff.

GA1502

Experimenting with Carbonated Water
Soda Springs, Idaho–Start of Hudspeth Cutoff

Near Soda Springs where the Hudspeth Cutoff started, there were many mineral springs that amazed the emigrants. Some were hot springs and some very cold. Their taste varied, depending on their mineral content. Some even made noises. Chester Ingersoll in a letter in 1847 described some of the springs as being warm and loaded with iron, sulphur, soda, and lime. He also described Steamboat, the most famous spring. It was foaming and had a temperature of 88°F (31°C). Periodically it threw water five or six feet (1.5 or 1.8 m) in the air. Ten feet (3 m) away was an opening where steam escaped. In the area he felt there were one hundred or more springs. Most of these springs today are under the waters of Soda Point Reservoir, which was formed when the Bear River was dammed.

The springs were mentioned in almost every diary of an emigrant who passed this way. Joe Sharp wrote (1852): "By sweetening the water of those springs it made very fine drinks; one of them we considered superior to the others. Steamboat Spring emitted puffs of steam at intervals that sounded similar to the puffing of an engine on a steamboat." Rufus Sage wrote (1849): ". . . theare is over a hundred of them they ar on the bank of the bear river the water when you first dip it up sparkles and fomes the same as sodo it also tasts like sodo water only a great deal stronger . . . ." William J.J. Scott (1846) wrote in a letter: "the Sody Spring is aquite acuriosity thare is agreat many of them Just boiling rite up out of the groung take alitle sugar and desolve it in alittle water and then dip up acup full and drink it before it looses it gass it is fristrate I drank ahal of galon of it you will see several Spring Spouting up out ove the river it is quite asite to see."

Hooper Spring can be visited today in a city park. It is an oval-shaped pool and is covered with a pavilion roof. Local residents of the area sometimes drink this water, but it is better if a little Tang is added. James Wilkins wrote (1849): "we took our tin cups and some sugar and drank repeated draughts of excellent soda water." One emigrant felt it tasted better if it was made into coffee. He found that his horse refused to drink the water but would drink coffee made from it! Some found that the water was naturally carbonated enough to raise bread!

GA1502

Experimenting with Carbonated Water Activity

The sparkling waters of these springs contain minerals and carbon dioxide. You can learn about density while experimenting with carbon dioxide.

1. Fill a glass jar with water. Stir in about $1/3$ cup of vinegar and two teaspoons of baking soda. Stir slowly and carefully so the mixture doesn't froth too much. (You can also use a chilled, colorless, carbonated beverage such as club soda, 7-Up™, or Alka Seltzer™.)

2. Add a few raisins to the fizzy liquid. It is better if they are a bit dry and hard. This could also be done with uncooked popcorn or macaroni.

3. Observe the raisins. At first they will sink to the bottom, but after a little while, each one will rise to the surface and spin a bit—but they will not stay there! They will keep sinking to the bottom and bouncing up again for several hours.

4. Here is what is happening: The raisins are more dense than the liquid and sink when dropped into the glass. The bubbles are the carbon dioxide gas, like that found in the mineral springs. It is formed when vinegar and baking soda join together in a chemical reaction. This is the same gas that makes the bubbles in fizzy drinks. When the raisins are on the bottom of the glass, they are collecting carbon dioxide bubbles which form at the bottom of the glass. Together, the bubbles and raisins are less dense than the liquid, so the raisins are lifted to the surface. At the surface, the bubbles break and the gases are released to the air. As the bubbles are released, the raisin spins if there are more bubbles on one side of the raisin. After losing the bubbles, the density of the raisin becomes greater and it sinks. On the bottom, they soon collect more bubbles and bounce up again. The process is repeated again and again.

GA1502

Silent City of Rocks
Almo, Idaho

The Silent City of Rocks was a very important location because it was the junction of the three main California emigrant routes. The Fort Hall-Raft River Route and the Hudspeth Cutoff trails came into the Silent City of Rocks from the north, and the Salt Lake Trail entered the area at the southern end near the famous Steeple Rock (known as the Twin Sisters today).

The area was also important because the emigrants were so interested in the unusual rock formations throughout this valley. The huge rocks found in the area reminded the emigrants of buildings they had known or could imagine. They often painted building names on the rocks such as City Hotel or Castle Rock. The valley also went by names such as Pyramid Valley and Valley of the Rocks.

California emigrant journals almost always had comments about the Silent City of Rocks. Goldsborough Bruff wrote (1849): "We entered a very extraordinary valley, called the 'CITY OF CASTLES.'. . . A couple of miles long and probably 1/2 mile broad. A light grey . . . granite . . . in blocks of every size . . . The travellers had marked several large blocks . . . On one was marked (with tar) 'NAPOLEON'S CASTLE,' another 'CITY HOTEL,' &c. We nooned among these curious monuments of nature. I dined hastily on bread and water, and while others rested, I explored and sketched some of these queer rocks. A group . . . resembled gigantic fungii, petrified, others clusters were worn in cells and caverns and one . . . seemed no larger than a big chest, was, to my astonishment when close to it, quite large, hollow, with an arched entrance, and capable of containing a dozen persons . . . ."

Even though many of the journals recorded the wonders of nature at the Silent City of Rocks, the stories of the struggling of some pioneers were also written down. For example, Joseph Middleton wrote about his wagon train having to leave a family behind and not giving them any food (1849): ". . . We parted with poor Kinaw and his wife and 3 children and refused him 50 lbs. of flour–May God be merciful and take care of them in this inhospitable country. Some of the Wolverine Rangers (a company of 21 wagons) have come up while I was writing at this last creek. They seem to have shown more humanity to Mr. Kinaw than our Co.–one of them told me that they had given him a bag of meal . . . ."

GA1502

Newsreel Storytelling of the California Trail
Silent City of Rocks

At the Silent City of Rocks, many emigrants tried to describe the wonders of the area in their journals. They found it hard to find words that adequately described the unusual rock formations. For example, John Steele wrote (1850): ". . . At the western base of the mountain we caught a glimpse of what at first appeared to be a city of ruins. There were the walls, domes, monuments, spires, palaces, and roofs, all of dazzling white . . . Here were pyramids of white granite . . . rocks in the form of castles with domes and turrets, spires rising probably five hundred feet, and nicely balanced on the point of some of them large pieces of granite . . . the wild mountain background, the clear, cold streams and flower-decked meadows, presented a scene over which one would delight to linger, and yet find it difficult to describe."

Leander Loomis wrote (1850): "To wander among these vast ledges of rocks, to crawl in the great caves, caverns, and holes, which nature has formed in these rocks fills the mind of man, with a wild romantic Grandeur . . . causes man to Gaze with astonishment, and wonder, at natures doing. In fact, nature has displayed herself with such perfection that Language cannot describe its beauties . . . therefore you must imagine for yourselves the thoughts of the traveller, as he thus wanders far from home in a wild uninhabited, yet majestic and beautiful land."

James F. Wilkins was a St. Louis artist who headed to California in 1849. He was one of the first to use "City of Rocks" to name the area. It was hard to describe this area with words, but some, like Wilkins, tried to do it through paintings. By following the Gold Rush, he made sketches that he later made into a huge moving panoramic painting which he exhibited. A "panorama" is a picture that is shown a part at a time by being unrolled in front of the audience. Wilkins charged admission for people to see his moving painting. It was like a newsreel of its day. His painting was very popular with the public but was only on display for a few years in the St. Louis area. The painting is now gone, but his field sketches have survived.

GA1502

Newsreel Storytelling of the California Trail Activity

Like Wilkins, you can make a type of pioneer newsreel.

1. Cut a large window out of the bottom of a cardboard box to make the box look like a television. Paint and add other decorations so the box looks like a television set.

2. Get a fairly long roll of paper that has a width that will fit inside the box. (The window that has been cut in the box needs to be just slightly smaller than the width of the paper.)

3. On the roll of paper, draw and color a collection of California Trail pictures, scene by scene. When the paper is unrolled, the scenes will appear in the window of the "television" in an appropriate order and the correct size. Draw large enough and dark enough so your audience can easily understand what they are seeing. Use paints, crayons, or felt pens. Draw pictures of what it was like for the emigrants on the California Trail. Imagine that they really had television in those days. The pictures you draw are what the people in the East would see of life on the trail such as cooking and hunting. They could also be of landscapes and scenery, such as the unusual Silent City of Rocks.

4. Cut slits into the box for the paper to pass through. The slits need to be cut into the two sides of the box adjoining the side with the window, and very close to the window. Pull the paper through the slits so that one scene at a time will show in the window. It will be easier if you have two wooden dowels to attach to each end of the paper roll so you can neatly roll up the paper as you give your presentation.

5. This can also be made from a sturdy shoe box, on a smaller scale. The window would be cut out of the bottom of the shoe box. If the window is small enough, a roll of adding machine tape can be used for the roll of paper, but the pictures would have to be drawn very small. The paper could be rolled up on pencils instead of wooden dowels.

6. Write a script of what you want to tell the audience about each picture. Include accurate facts and interesting stories of the California Trail. Arrange your writing in the same order as your pictures are on the roll of paper.

7. Practice first and then perform your "Newsreel of the California Trail" to an audience. If you would like, you could add commercials that you think would have been appropriate for that time in history.

22

GA1502

Silent City of Rocks to the Humboldt River
Almo, Idaho, to Humboldt Divide Near Wells, Nevada

With the three main branches of the California Trail–Raft River-Fort Hall, Salt Lake Trail, and Hudspeth Cutoff–all back together at the Silent City of Rocks, the trail continued on through Junction Valley. In the valleys between the Raft River and the Humboldt River, they usually found good water and grass for their cattle. The surrounding hills, though, were desert-like with sparse grass, sagebrush, and prickly pear cactus.

They next came to Granite Pass with its difficult and dangerous descent to Goose Creek. Except for South Pass, this pass received more emigrant traffic than any other pass on the route to California. It was much more difficult and dramatic than South Pass, but it has almost been forgotten. Joseph Middleton described the steep descent (1849): ". . . up some steeps, but more commonly down very steep and twisting places . . . On coming down this hill saw 2 dead oxen . . . The last hill . . . is so steep and bad, that the driver, a man of good judgment . . . said it was the worst since we left Independence . . . ."

Alonzo Delano described the Goose Creek Valley through which they traveled (1849): "Our route to-day was through a narrow vale, . . . occasionally opening into basins, with high bare and rocky mountains around us. The hills were either white with lime, or presented the bleak aspect of the black trap-rocks in high and perpendicular cliffs. We passed several springs which were so warm that the hand could hardly be borne in them; yet within a few feet of one was a spring of pure, cold water . . . ." Delano laughed at himself as he wrote about traveling along this part of the trail: ". . . I attempted to jump across a narrow stream, but like thousands of others in the world, I missed my mark, and fell into the water . . . although I 'looked before I leaped.' Squash, squash–I had my boots full of water, and should have drank it with pleasure . . . ."

Travel was monotonous. For many of the emigrants, this stretch of trail is where they really began to miss their families. William Swain wrote (1849): "This morning I left camp on the pony ahead of the train. We were in a large mountain plain . . . The sun had just risen above the eastern range of brown and rolling hills . . . Indian summer brought fresh to my mind those days, that home with its relatives and its friends. I can but think of happy hours spent in their society at my peaceful and happy home. I have thought much of my wife and child lately, and it appears hard to be deprived of their society so long . . . ."

GA1502

Settling Quarrels on the Trail Activity
Silent City of Rocks to the Humboldt River

There were bound to be quarrels among the emigrants as they lived and worked so closely together for so many months. Along the Goose Creek Valley, Byron McKinstry wrote about an argument he was involved in (1850): "Tuttle and I had a few angry words at our camp this morning. It was Tuttle's and my week to cook, but for a long time past he had been in the habit of laying in bed and letting me get the breakfast alone. I took occasion to say something about it this morning to Blackman so loud as to be heard by T. in the tent. He resented it and soon let us know that he was not sleeping as he generally pretended to be. One word led to another till at last he threatened to strike me. I replied that it would be well for him to let [hire] that job out, if he wished to go to Cal. Such threats are foolish to say the least. We were good friends again after breakfast. I will call this Quarrel Camp."

Consider other things the emigrants might have argued about along the California Trail.

1. Fill out the chart, using more paper if needed.

List Jobs to Be Done Along the Trail	What Might the People Have Argued About Concerning This Specific Job?

2. Choose one of the jobs/arguments that you have listed on the chart. In a conversational style, write a series of arguments back and forth between two emigrants, about the job. The conversation should end with resolving their argument. Give the emigrants names. Use proper conversation format such as indenting for each new speaker, using proper commas, proper quotation marks, and correct spelling.

Following the Humboldt River
Wells, Nevada, to Ryepatch Reservoir, Nevada

The longest stretch of the California Trail was the section that followed the Humboldt River. This winding river flowed 390 miles across dry flatlands that lay between the mountain ranges of the Great Basin. The California Trail probably could not have existed without this river and its life-giving grass for the animals. Fremont changed the name from Mary's River to the Humboldt. It was named for Baron von Humboldt, a famous naturalist.

The trail was not difficult, but it was a very long, dusty, boring, hot stretch of trail. An emigrant from the Stevens party wrote (1844): "The journey down the Humboldt was very monotonous. Each day's events were substantially a repetition of those of the day before."

Due to the high elevation of about 4000 feet (1219 m), there were extremes in temperature. James Wilkins wrote (1849): "This is I think one of the most detestable countries God ever made, to say nothing of its sterility and barrenness. The nights are so cold we cannot keep warm in bed, ice forms every night . . . While the middle of the day the sun pours down his beams, and the heat is as oppressive as at St. Louis." To escape the heat, many emigrants rested during the day and traveled at night so the trail was almost as busy in the dark! The coolness of the evenings helped the half-starved cattle but even so, they often collapsed from overwork.

Gravelly Ford was where the emigrants crossed to the south side of the Humboldt for the first time. From this point, all the way to the Humboldt Sink, trails followed both sides of the river. James Pritchard wrote (1849): ". . . We reached the river by 2 PM–swam our mules across to grass. We found a luxury here such as we had not before seen, in the shape of the wild currens [currents]. There was the black yellow & red. The flavor of them was very fine indeed. We had as a rarity today, a fine pleasant shower of rain."

Food was not always this easy to get. Byron McKinstry described a man who asked to buy food from them (1850): ". . . Before we had done our breakfast a very gentlemanly looking man came up with a pack on his back and very politely asked us if we would sell him a little flour or bread . . . He had eaten nothing lately but a little beef. His last horse died on the Salt desert. Those that have money can buy a little poor beef, but nothing else . . . I presume that twenty men per day apply to us for food, most of them without money. These must eat horses and carrion I am afraid. There must be a great deal of suffering on the road yet."

For about three weeks the emigrants followed the monotonous Humboldt River. Reuben Shaw described this river (1849): "The reader should not imagine the Humboldt to be a rapid mountain stream, with its cool and limpid waters rushing down the rocks of steep inclines, with here and there beautiful cascades and shady pools under mountain evergreens, where the sun never intrudes and where the speckled trout loves to sport . . . the Humboldt is not fit for man nor beast . . . There is not a fish nor any other living thing to be found in its waters, and there is not timber enough in three hundred miles of its desolate valley to make a snuffbox, or sufficient vegetation along its banks to shade a rabbit, while its waters contain the alkali to make soap for a nation, and after winding its sluggish way through a desert . . . it sinks, disappears . . . ."

Leander Loomis described the journey along the Humboldt as "getting a peep at the Elliphant," meaning difficult times were starting (1850): "A word for Old Humboldt . . . we find a crooked muddy stream, with a wide and swampy bottom so much so that it is utterly impossible to get horses in to the river at scarcely any point, the road is obliged to keep out among the hills, the valley being impassible from the fact of its being, so muddy. The road all along this river, is so dusty, that is makes travelling very disagreeable . . . the dust along this river is from one to six to eight inches deep, being of the very lightest kind, so that the least wind will stir it up, and almost blind a person. I have seen it so thick that we could not see wagons that were . . . ahead."

Dust was a continual problem along the Humboldt. Alonzo Delano wrote (1849): "One of the most disagreable things in traveling through this country is the smothering clouds of dust. The soil is parched by the sun, and the earth is reduced to a . . . powder by the long trains of wagons, while the sage bushes prevent the making of new tracks. Generally we had a strong wind blowing from the west, and there was no getting rid of the dust. We literally had to eat, drink, and breathe it . . . ."

James Clyman (1846): "[wind] shifted and blew up such a dust that the sun was completely obscured all the afternoon . . . whirlwinds . . . carry large quantities [of dust] to a great height resembling a white smoke . . . ."

Israel Hale added some humor as he wrote (1849): ". . . as yet we have not been the least troubled with them (mosquitoes). I cannot account for it in any other way than, judging from my own feeling, that they cannot stand the dust."

GA1502

Build a River Model Activity

Shaw wrote that "With the exception of a short distance near its source it has the least perceptible current." Even though the Humboldt had little current, all rivers cut away at the land to some degree. You can build a model of a river showing this erosion process.

1. Wash out three empty half-gallon milk cartons. Cut out the side panel of each carton under the spout, but leave the spout. Take the milk cartons outside for this project.

2. Lay the first milk carton on its side with the open, cutout side up. Set the other two cartons aside. Fill the carton about half full of wet soil. The soil level should be even with the open spout. Smooth the surface of the soil. In order to make a river that flows, place a rock or clay (1 cm high) under the end of the carton that is away from the spout.

3. Fill a two-liter bottle with water. Place the mouth of the bottle on the edge of the higher end of the carton. Slowly pour all the water on the soil, keeping an even, constant flow. A small stream of water should flow over the surface of the soil and out the spout. Observe what happens to the water and to the formation of the river in the soil. Look at the shape of the river that is cut and its depth.

4. Repeat steps 2 and 3 with the other milk cartons. However, with the second one, raise one end 3 cm high. With the third carton, raise it 5 cm high. Observe the differences and similarities between the three rivers that are created. As the slope of the carton is increased, what happens to the depth of the river that is formed? If possible, get more milk cartons and try this again, using different types of soil, such as sandy soil or soil that is mostly clay. Observe the differences and similarities with the different soil types. Try collecting the water that comes out the spout and comparing the runoff with each type of river. What is in the water? Why?

5. Which "milk carton rivers" seem most like the Humboldt River? Why?

GA1502

Hastings Cutoff
Salt Lake City, Utah, to Near Elko, Nevada, at Carlin Canyon on the Humboldt River

Lansford Hastings grew restless as an Ohio lawyer and decided to travel West. In 1842 he journeyed to Oregon and then moved south to California. At that time, California was ruled by what Hastings thought was a very weak Mexican government. He felt that the Americans could revolt, like they had done in Texas. California could become an independent republic. Although it didn't work out this way, Hastings thought he could be the President. This plan would work only if he could convince more American settlers to come to California.

In 1844 he returned to the United States, and in 1845 he published a book called *The Emigrants' Guide to Oregon and California*. The purpose of his book was to convince emigrants to come West. He made the journey sound very easy. He explained that the route to Fort Hall was north of the most direct route to California. It would be shorter to travel southwest from Fort Bridger to the Great Salt Lake and then go west across the desert to the Humboldt River. He talked to John Fremont, an explorer; studied the trail on pack mules; and felt he could bring emigrants across what became known at Hastings Cutoff.

In 1846 he arrived at Fort Bridger in time to persuade some of the emigrants to try his shortcut to California. Even though wagons had never taken that route, he felt they would have no more difficulty than the mules. Emigrants who felt they were behind schedule were more easily convinced to try a shortcut. Among the last to be convinced was the group that became known as the Donner Party.

Hastings went as a guide with the first wagons that wanted to try the shortcut. They traveled down the rugged Echo Canyon to the Weber River, towards what is today Salt Lake City. It was a very difficult trip down the canyon, and some of the wagons had to travel right in the river. It had been such a bad experience that Hastings returned a few miles and left a note to the other wagons that were coming. It said that if they sent a messenger, Hastings would return and guide them along a better route, but he didn't keep his word. When the Donner Party found the note, James Reed rode ahead to get help, but Hastings would only ride to a high spot in the mountains and vaguely point to a better route. The Donner Party got further and further behind.

After the groups were through the Wasatch Mountains, they traveled around the south shore of the Great Salt Lake. The route then turned sharply southward and left the lake. There were springs with good water and grass, but after this there would be no more water on the desert. They had first been told the distance across the desert would be forty miles (56.4 km) or might even be avoided altogether. They were now told to prepare for two days and two nights without water. This would be a disaster for the cattle! They filled all the water containers they had, even their coffeepots and boots. Some filled their waterproof oilcloth pants with water, tied tightly at the ankles. They cut all the grass they could carry in the wagons.

GA1502

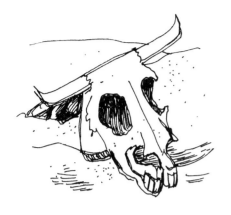

Soon the oxen were tired and suffering from thirst and hunger. Samuel Young wrote (1846): "Such a sight! The sun rose in full splendor, reflecting his rays on this vast salt plain, as white as snow, and as far as the eye could reach not a thing to be seen, not a spear of grass or a drop of water. Oxen gave out and lay down, some to rise no more; others from extreme thirst, became crazy and nothing could be done with them, and finally they would become exhausted and drop down dead. Wagons were abandoned until it seemed as if all were lost." Henry Bloom described the desert, ". . . our water all gone and our horses nearly famishing for water. Teams giving out, men lying by the side of the road in the hot sun speechless for the want of water . . . Men offering one, ten, twenty and five hundred dollars for a single drink of water . . . ." Most groups that chose this route eventually had to leave the women and children in the wagons and take the animals ahead to find water and grass near Pilot Peak. Some people were black-tongued and bleeding from the mouth when they staggered to the spring beneath Pilot Peak. When the animals were strong enough to travel, they went back across the desert to get the wagons and families. The distance across the desert was at least eighty miles (129 km), rather than forty (56 km). An ox team that moved two miles (3.2 km) an hour, without stopping to rest, would have taken forty-one and a half hours to make the desert crossing!

Hastings made another mistake after they passed Pilot Peak. If they had traveled north for a day over fairly easy land, they would have reached the Humboldt River. Unfortunately, the Ruby Mountains blocked their way west, and they had a long detour to the south, eventually rejoining the main California Trail along the Humboldt. They were very frustrated when they learned that for all of their hardships, they had not been on a shortcut at all. They had lost time, instead, and they were behind the people who had taken the main trail. The Hastings Cutoff got a bad reputation and was soon not traveled much.

Stitching a Guidebook
Hastings Cutoff

Emigrants planning trips to the West needed help knowing what trail conditions would be like, what equipment to take, and how to find their way. Some learned this information from letters from friends who had already gone to California. Some people sold "road directions," handwritten (and later printed) on single sheets of paper. Emigrants also relied on guidebooks that had been written specifically to describe the journey. For example, Lansford Hastings wrote *The Emigrants' Guide to Oregon and California* in 1845. Even though he had made several trips, the guide was neither detailed nor reliable. He made the trip seem much easier than it was because he was trying to convince emigrants to move West.

After gold was discovered in California in 1848, many more guidebooks were printed. For example, one of the better guidebooks was written by Joseph Ware, called *The Emigrants' Guide to California*. Its subtitle listed its contents: "containing every point of information for the emigrant–including routes, distances, water, grass, timber, crossing of rivers, passes, altitudes, with a large map of routes, and profile of country, &c.,–with full directions for testing and assaying gold and other ores." An example of its practical advice was about travel hours. It advised, "Start at 4–travel till the sun gets high–camp till the heat is over. Then start again and travel till dark."

Most of these guidebooks contained a lot of fiction and exaggeration. For example, *The Emigrants' Guide to the Gold Mines* told of riverbeds "paved with gold to the thickness of a hand," from which "twenty to fifty thousand dollars of gold" could be "picked out almost instantly." Most guidebooks borrowed heavily from newspaper articles, hearsay, and from earlier journals.

Stitching a Guidebook Activity

Stitching and writing a guidebook lets you share your knowledge with others.

1. Fold (at least) four sheets of 8½" x 11" (21.6 x 27.94 cm) paper in half. On the inside fold, make five evenly spaced small dots, in pencil. Have a partner hold your book. Push a pin through each dot and back out again. This will mark your stitching holes.

2. Stitch the book with fish line, yarn, embroidery floss, or regular thread. Cut the thread about five times the distance between the first and last holes. Use a single strand of thread and do not tie a knot. Using a large needle, stitch the book with the traditional five-hole stitch. This is a stitch that has been done by many generations of bookbinders. (It can be done with any odd number of holes.) Start the stitching going down through the center hole on the back, outside side. When the stitching is done, end with a bow (or knot) on the back, outside side.

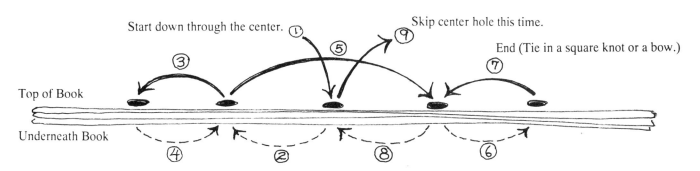

3. **Write a guidebook on one of these choices:**
   a. Imagine that you were a trail expert back in the days of the California Trail. Write a guidebook for the emigrants.
   b. Write a guidebook for someone from faraway coming to visit your city, state, or county this year.

   For either of these types of books, give advice to the travelers such as what they should take with them, routes of travel, climate/temperatures, landmarks to see, and maps.

4. **Fill your pages in this order:**
   a. When writing your book, leave the front and back inside covers blank.
   b. Make your first regular page a title page that tells the name of the book, author's name, and date it was written.
   c. On the next nine pages write your guidebook information.
   d. As a title on the next to the last page write this heading: Comments from the Readers. Leave the rest of the page blank. When the book is finished, have people who read your book write positive comments about it.
   e. As a title on the last page write this heading: About the Author. Do not write this information in "first person." For example, say: *John Jones* wrote this California Trail guidebook to help emigrants. Don't say: *I* wrote this California Trail guidebook to help emigrants.
   f. After your have finished your book, write a title on the outside. Also, put a colored picture on your cover. When you are finished, proofread your book for accuracy and neatness. Then share your book with other people and collect their comments.

Following the Lower Humboldt River
Ryepatch Reservoir to the Humboldt Sink, Nevada

Lassen's Meadows was a broad grasslands along the Humboldt River at today's Ryepatch Reservoir. Here the emigrants had the choice of continuing to follow the Humboldt River south or to head west over the Lassen-Applegate Trail. Both routes crossed the mountains into California.

At Lassen's Meadows there were so many trails that it was almost like a maze. Since it was so easy to get confused, the place was sometimes called Fool's Meadow. One man described seeing two hundred wagons going every which way at the same time, as each driver tried to find the correct route. As people tried to decide which route to take, there were always rumors about the trails. People would say the main California Trail had a dangerous desert crossing, that there were impassable mountains, and that the grass along the Lower Humboldt had already been eaten. They would say the Applegate-Lassen route also had a desert, that the Indians were hostile, that there was little water or grass, and that it was a longer route through the mountains. Regardless of which way they went, the remaining miles to the Sacramento Valley would be long and difficult.

The main California Trail continued on to the south, following the Lower Humboldt River. It continued to be hot and bleak. One emigrant woman wrote that she was "obliged to swallow dust all day in place of water. I have suffered more this afternoon than all my sufferings put together."

At the Humboldt Sink the river ended in a marshy, swampy meadow with small salt lakes. There was plenty of grass and water for the animals. The emigrants usually rested here a day or two to make preparations for their difficult days ahead crossing the Sierras.

At one time this area east of the Sierras had much more rain. Also, during the Pleistocene Era, beginning one million years ago, there were changes in the earth's climate. Large glaciers grew and receded in the Sierras. Waters from these melting glaciers filled the desert basins and formed many large lakes. They got deeper and deeper and eventually overflowed to form one gigantic lake. Geologists have named this great prehistoric lake Lake Lahontan. At one time it covered over 9000 square miles! Gradually the climate became warmer and the water evaporated faster than the lake refilled. Eventually the one huge lake became many smaller lakes again. The last two remaining lakes today are Pyramid Lake and Walker Lake. Other lake bottoms became alkali flats and various sinks, such as the Humboldt Sink.

GA1502

Writing Letters to Friends Back on the Trail
Following the Lower Humboldt River

At the junction where the Applegate-Lassen Trail joins the main California Trail, emigrants often left notes and letters for friends who were yet to come that way. They told what route they had chosen, as well as telling news. Edwin Banks wrote (1849): ". . . Saw the road to the right, determined not to take it. A host of notes left here for friends; lines on cards and boards, all open for general inspection . . . Why, taking this or that road, state of health, condition of cattle, and company. Some of them well written; others, the schoolmaster certainly was abroad . . . ." Simon Doyle observed (1849): ". . . At the forks were various posts and boards covered with notices from persons ahead to their friends behind saying which road they had gone on. Several trains were there; men quarreling about which way they should go; women and children crying. We hurried on to get away from the busel [bustle]."

J. Goldsborough Bruff wrote (1849): ". . . in the forks of the road, I observed a red painted barrel standing.–I rode up, to examine it.–It was a nice new barrel, about the size of a whisky-barrel, iron hoops, and a square hole cut in the head; and neatly painted in black block letters, upon it, "POST OFFICE." On looking in, I found it half-full of letters, notes, notices, &c.–Near this was a stick and billboard, also filled with notices.–These were chiefly directed to emigrants in the rear, hurrying them along, giving information about route, telling who had taken this or the southern route. &c. . . . I inscribed a card and left, here, for the benefit of all whom it might concern, as follows:–

'The Washington City Company.
Capt Bruff, pass'd–on the
right-hand trail, Septr
19th. 2 p.m. 1849.'"

Apparently, most emigrants dumped the letters out of the barrel, read all the letters, and then added some letters of their own. Many journals mention receiving letters from these "self-help post offices."

Writing Letters to Friends Back on the Trail Activity

Pretend you are an emigrant. Write a letter that could have been written to a friend (or relative) who was traveling behind you on the trail. This note would be left at Lassen's Meadows to tell this friend which direction you had gone and any news of your family and travels.

1. Write down some notes about you and your emigrant family:
   Give yourself an emigrant-sounding name. Decide who your friends and family members are. Tell what kind of animals you have and how many wagons. Write down some things that have happened to your family as you've traveled along the Humboldt River. Decide whether you will continue following the Humboldt River to the south on the main California Trail or whether you will go west on the Applegate-Lassen Trail.

2. Using your notes as a guide, write a short letter to a friend (or relative) who is behind you on the trail. Write this in the correct "friendly letter" format, like that found in an English book. After you've written your letter, smear a little mud or dust on the paper and crumple and tear it a bit so it looks as if it's been sitting out in the harsh desert, waiting to be picked up. If you are doing this as a class, you might want to create a bulletin board of a desert scene–sand, sagebrush, a little grass, the sluggish Humboldt River, and dark mountains. Draw some posts and boards (or the "Post Office" barrel like Bruff described). Each of you attach your emigrant letters to the posts and boards.

Example of the friendly letter format:
(**Note:** The top line was added to show what would have been put on the front of the letter since they would not have had envelopes. It's not standard friendly letter format.)

Letter for Elizabeth Williams:

Sept. 5, 1849

Dear Elizabeth,

   I miss you very much and hope you are not far behind us. Were your days along the Humboldt River as boring, hot, and dusty as ours?...............................
....
....

Your friend,
Mary

34

Forty Mile Desert
Humboldt Sink to the Beginning Climb up the Sierras

The Forty Mile Desert started a few miles beyond the Humboldt Sink. A Nevada historical marker states: "The 40 Mile Desert . . . is a barren stretch of waterless alkali wasteland. It was the most dreaded section of the California Emigrant Trail. If possible, it was traveled at night because of the great heat . . . Regardless of its horrors, it became the accepted route." The Truckee Route went west across the desert, and the Carson and Sonora routes crossed the desert to the south.

Emigrants were glad to leave the monotonous Humboldt River, but the Forty Mile Desert was a very difficult stretch of trail. It was especially hard because it came so near the end of the journey, when supplies were low, the animals were weak, and the wagons were in poor condition. The soft surface of the deep sand made it hard for the struggling oxen to pull the wagons. The choking dust and intense heat caused great misery. One of the guidebooks described the trail after the Humboldt Sink: ". . . From this place to the [Truckee] river the distance is forty miles, and must be performed in one stretch, as there is no grass nor good water on the road . . . ." Traveling the desert took from two to four days, with just brief stops to rest the animals.

Charles True wrote (1859): ". . . The glass-like sandhills reflected the heat and the sun's dazzling rays like so many mirrors. The sand for a time was uncomfortably hot to the feet, and our faithful dog's worn and cracked feet caused him to sit up on his haunches and cry like a child with pains . . . Here was to be, by far, the most strenuous test of endurance to which our animals had been subjected . . . We had always endeavored to treat them well . . . It was only natural that we had become strongly attached to them. We had walked by their sides and watched day by day their familiar forms as though members of our family . . . our poor animals were beginning to feel the effects of the heat and the need of water greatly . . . Our feelings were touched as they constantly looked at us, as if entreating for water and food. They were panting rapidly, and their long protruding tongues hung from their open mouths. We finally stopped briefly to give them each a small quantity of water from our scanty supply. They, at once, lay down on the hot sand even though still yoked and hitched to the wagon. When it came time for us to move on, they required much urging to get them on their feet and started off again . . . ."

Many of the emigrants' personal items had to be thrown out to lighten the wagons. Margaret Frink wrote (1850): "For many weeks we had been accustomed to see property abandoned and animals dead or dying. But those scenes were here doubled and trebled . . . Both sides of the road for miles were lined with dead animals and abandoned wagons. Around them were strewed yokes, chains, harness, guns, tools, bedding, clothing, cooking-utensils, and many other articles, in utter confusion . . . But no one stopped to gaze or help. The living procession marched steadily onward, giving little heed to the destruction going on, in their own anxiety to reach a place of safety. In fact, the situation was so desperate that, in most cases, no one could help another. Each had all he could do to save himself and his animals."

Henrietta Catherine McDaniel also wrote about the hardships (1853): ". . . it was to be an all-night trek. It might well have been named 'Death's trail,' for as we followed the winding trail through the sagebrush, we saw white bones and carcasses of various animals . . . About two o'clock in the morning, we came up to a very light cart-wagon drawn by two oxen, both of which were lying down while hitched to the wagon. On a quilt by the side of the cart lay a man, woman and two children. They had completely given out and were sick and starving."

There was no grass and no drinkable water except the mineral-filled Boiling Springs that they reached about halfway across the desert. It helped if men were sent ahead on horseback to dam part of the springs so the water would be cool enough for the oxen to drink. The springs were a curiosity to the emigrants. Some boiled high like geysers and some gurgled and steamed. Eliza Ann McAuley wrote (1852): "These springs boil up with great noise, emitting a very nauseous smell . . . We hear that a woman and child have got scalded very badly by stepping into one of them."

They had dreaded this desert crossing and once over it, were very relieved. John Steele wrote, upon reaching the Truckee River: ". . . luxury once more to recline beneath the shadow of a tree . . . [Emigrants] ragged, dusty, weary, and starved they come . . . with bruised, blistered, and bleeding feet, plodding through the hot sand . . . ."

GA1502

Why There Is a Desert East of the Sierra Mountains
Forty Mile Desert

The Forty Mile Desert caused great hardships among the emigrants. Sallie Hester wrote about her difficulties crossing the desert (1849): "Stopped and cut grass for the cattle and supplied ourselves with water for the desert [at Humboldt Sink]. Had a trying time crossing. Several of our cattle gave out, and we left one. Our journey through the desert was from Monday, three o'clock in the afternoon, until Thursday morning at sunrise, September 6. The weary journey last night, the mooing of the cattle for water, their exhausted condition, with the cry of 'Another ox down,' the stopping of the train to unyoke the poor dying brute, to let him follow at will or stop by the wayside and die, and the weary, weary tramp of men and beasts, worn out with heat and famished for water, will never be erased from my memory. Just at dawn, in the distance, we had a glimpse of the Truckee River, and with it the feeling: Saved at last!"

The emigrants did not appreciate this desert near the end of their journey, when they were tired and would need energy to cross the Sierras. However, the desert's location exists for a good reason: The sun shines on the Pacific Ocean off the coast of California and some of the water evaporates. This warm air rises and carries the water vapor up with it, as it "climbs" up the west side of the Sierra Mountains. As this warm air rises, it gets colder. Cold air can't hold as much water vapor as warm air, so some of the water vapor turns back into water drops. This is called condensation. The water in the air changes from gas (water vapor) to liquid (water drops). Clouds are made of billions of tiny water drops. Each of these drops condenses on a bit of dust. The tiny drops slowly grow larger as more water vapor condenses. The bigger, heavier water drops begin to sink down through the clouds. As they go, they bump into other water drops and make bigger and bigger drops. (This can be seen with water drops on windows or on the bathroom mirror.) When the water drops become too big and heavy for the cloud to hold, they fall to the ground as rain. (Falling raindrops aren't really tear-shaped. They are rounded on top and flattened on the bottom, more like the shape of hamburger buns.)

This rain falls on the west side of the Sierras. There is very little moisture left in the clouds after they have passed over the mountains, so little rain can fall on the east side of the Sierras. This is called the "rain shadow effect." This lack of rainfall created the Forty Mile Desert. (This same effect happens with the Cascade Mountains in Oregon and Washington, causing the land on the east side of the mountains to be very dry. The emigrants on the Oregon Trail also had to cross dry desert lands, but they weren't quite as difficult to cross.)

GA1502

Why There Is a Desert East of the Sierra Mountains Activity

Try this activity to show the rain shadow effect.

1. On a warm day, find a hill that you can run up.

2. Fill a bucket or #10 can completely full of water.

3. Put the bucket at the bottom of the hill.

4. With a friend, pick up the bucket. Each person holds onto the handle with only one hand. The bucket is like a cloud.

5. Both people run quickly up the hill, each continuing to hold the bucket with only one hand.

6. Much of the water will spill out by the time the top of the hill is reached. There will be little water left that could be dumped on the other side of the hill. This shows the rain shadow effect. It's like the clouds losing most of their moisture by the time they reach the top of the Sierras and having little moisture left to dump on the other side. Therefore, the west side of the Sierras is much wetter than the east side.

A cloud can be made in a jar in this way.

1. With the help of an adult, pour very hot water in a jar or drinking glass. The water should fill the glass about $1/4$ full. This represents the water in the warm Pacific Ocean (although it really isn't this hot). The water in the ocean may not feel warm, but it is warmer than the air.

2. Set a dish of ice cubes on the top of the jar (no lid). This represents the colder air that is found at higher elevations, such as high in the Sierras.

3. A cloud will start to form in the jar. This happens when some of the water evaporates, forming a gas (water vapor). As it rises, it will be cooled. Cold air can't hold as much water vapor, so it will condense back into water drops. As it condenses, gradually it will "rain" down the inside sides of the jar. If it is not easy to see the cloud, try shaking a very small amount of dust off a chalkboard eraser into the jar. This will provide dust particles for the water drops to cling to.

Here are two easy ways to show condensation.

1. Since $2/3$ of human body weight is from water, every time a person breathes out, a little water vapor is put into the air. If the air is very cold, this water vapor condenses into little water drops. It can be seen as a white mist in front of the face.

2. Breathe out onto the surface of a mirror and watch it steam up. It's just like clouds. The mirror is colder than the air inside a person so when the air hits the mirror, the water in the air changes from gas to liquid.

GA1502

Indians of the Humboldt River Area
"Digger" Indians

The emigrants of the California Trail expected to have to fight Indians, but few ever did. The number of deaths was greatly exaggerated. Few journals tell of Indian hostilities. Journal research has shown that of the over 250,000 emigrants between 1840 and 1860, Indians killed 362. During that same period, emigrants killed 426 Indians. Sometimes it was the fear of an attack that caused a nervous pioneer to shoot first and cause trouble. Virginia Reed wrote (1846): "All the previous winter we were preparing for the journey and right here let me say that we suffered vastly more from fear of the Indians before starting than we did on the plains."

Most encounters with Indians were peaceful for the emigrants. Indians often acted as guides, traded game, and helped with river crossings. Margaret Frick wrote (1850): "In the afternoon we passed an Indian encampment . . . I had brought a supply of needles and thread, some of which I gave them. We also had some small mirrors in gilt frames, and a number of other trinkets, with which we could buy fish and fresh buffalo, deer, and antelope meat . . . ." The Indians were often hungry and came to the emigrant camps looking for food.

The emigrants called all the Indians from the Raft River to the Humboldt Sink, "Diggers." They dug in the ground for roots, grubs, and rodents to eat plus some of them dug holes in the ground for shelters. Although the different Indian tribes in this region had similar lifestyles because of living in the same environment, they were not all from one tribe or language group. The emigrants actually met Goshiutes, Paiutes, and Washoes. The Indians usually were not warlike during the early years of the emigration. The emigrants traveled down the Humboldt just once each year, in the late summer, and during these early years were not interested in the Indians' land. However, as the emigrants passed through, they killed or scared away the antelope and rabbits that the Indians needed for survival. These Indians had to live through the winter mostly on seeds which the women gathered during the summer. The oxen and mules of the emigrants ate the vegetation off before it could grow seeds. The passing of so many emigrants made it impossible for the Indians to gather seeds or fish along the river. They had no agriculture and were seminomadic as they moved with the seasons to find their food. The emigrants disrupted this ancient cycle of life.

Therefore, the Indians felt justified in stealing the animals of the emigrants, for revenge, for food, and because of their tradition of having little sense of private property. The emigrants had to guard their animals at night so they wouldn't be killed or stolen. Edwin Banks wrote (1849): "The Digger Indians . . . steal through necessity rather than choice." A few days later he added, ". . . The Indians have aroused a storm that may fall heavily on them. They stole eleven head of cattle here last night. One man who has a wife and seven children robbed of horses; his situation deplorable. This caused some twenty men to go well armed in pursuit of the Indians . . . ." The emigrants did not hold the Diggers in high regard. They were digusted that the Diggers ate anything they could find, including grasshoppers and rats. Fremont wrote (1843): "Roots, seeds, and grass, every vegetable that affords any nourishment, and every living animal thing, insect or worm, they eat . . . their sole employment is to obtain food; and they are constantly occupied in a struggle to support existence."

The Indian attacks shown in Western movies just didn't happen as they are portrayed. Indians didn't gallop around circled wagons, shooting arrows, while men fired their rifles from the shelter of the wagons. Attacking wagons in this way would have been too dangerous for the Indians. Instead, they tried to surprise single wagons that had been separated from the wagon train.

By 1857, the Indians had horses and guns and had grown bolder in their attacks on the emigrants. Early on the morning of August 13, a small group of emigrants that had camped by themselves were attacked by gunshots and arrows. One wounded man hid and several people were killed. The Indians found one remaining woman who was hiding in her tent in her nightgown. She had been shot with arrows. They thought she was dead so they scalped her. The Indians started to loot the wagons and steal the animals, but the approach of more wagons frightened them away. The wounded man then helped the scalped woman. In the haste of running away, the Indians had dropped her scalp. She found it and later had a wig made from her own hair. She never fully recovered from this frightening experience and eventually her mind failed. Though this was a horrible situation for the emigrants, they often treated the Indians terribly too. In frontier California, it was acceptable practice for soldiers to raid peaceful Indian reservations. Bounty hunters were well paid for Indian scalps. It was a situation that was doomed to violence. As more and more emigrants came West for land and treaties were broken, the Indians developed greater anxiety at being driven further from their traditional lands. There were no easy answers.

Comparing the Lives of the Emigrants and the Indians of the Humboldt Activity

It was obvious that when the emigrants moved west, there would be clashes between the cultures of the emigrants and the cultures of the Indians. In many ways, all groups of people are alike. In other ways, there are also differences between people of different cultures.

Fill in the chart to show the similarities and differences between the lives of the emigrants and the lives of the "Digger" Indians of the Humboldt River region. The similarities on this chart will show ways the two groups were alike. They might have been able to use these similarities to better understand each other. The differences on the chart will show why it was so hard for the two cultures to understand each other.

Ways the Two Groups' Lives Were Similar to Each Other (Alike)	Ways the Two Groups' Lives Were Different from Each Other (Not Alike)
Example: The emigrants and Indians both needed the wildlife for food.	Example: The emigrants had cattle, and the Indians of the Humboldt River region did not.

The Story of Sarah Winnemucca

Some sense of how the Paiutes felt about the emigrants can be found in a book by Sarah Winnemucca Hopkins called *Life Among the Piutes*, (older spelling of the tribe) published in 1883. She was the granddaughter of Chief Truckee who befriended and guided the Stevens Party in 1843 and remained a loyal friend of whites. She wrote about the encounters her people had with emigrants, as she had heard it through stories. She told of her father, Chief Winnemucca, who had gathered all the bands of Paiutes at the Carson Sink one spring and told them of one of his dreams. "These white people must be a great nation, as they have houses that move . . . I fear we will suffer greatly by their coming to our country; they come for no good to us, although my father said they were our brothers, but they do not seem to think we are like them. What do you all think about it? . . . " In his dream he saw more and more emigrants coming, with much bloodshed and the destruction of food. He hoped his people could hunt early that season before the wagons came. They needed to store much food in the mountains for the rest of the summer and for winter too.

The story of Sarah Winnemucca shows the misunderstandings that there were between the Indians and the emigrants. The families of both groups were afraid for their children. Sarah was probably born in 1844. In her book, she wrote about her childhood (1883) ". . . The following spring, before my grandfather returned home, there was a great excitement among my people . . . there was a fearful story they told us children. Our mothers told us that the whites were killing everybody and eating them. So we were all afraid of them. Every dust that we could see blowing in the valleys we would say it was the white people. In the late fall my father told his people to go to the rivers and fish, and we all went to Humboldt River, and the women went to work gathering wild seed, which they grind between the rocks . . . What a fright we all got one morning to hear some white people were coming. Every one ran as best they could . . . My aunt overtook us, and she said to my mother: 'Let us bury our girls, or we shall all be killed and eaten up.' So they went to work and buried us, and told us if we heard any noise not to cry out, for if we did they would surely kill us and eat us. So our mothers buried me and my cousin, planted sage bushes over our faces to keep the sun from burning them, and there we were left all day. Can any one imagine my feelings buried alive, thinking every minute that I was to be unburied and eaten up by the people that my grandfather loved so much? With my heart throbbing, and not daring to breathe, we lay there all day. It seemed that the night would never come . . . At last we heard some whispering. We did not dare to whisper to each other, so we lay still. I could hear their footsteps coming nearer and nearer. I thought my heart was coming right out of my mouth. Then I heard my mother say, 'T'is right here!' Oh, can any one in this world ever imagine what were my feelings when I was dug up by my poor mother and father . . . ?" Well, while we were in the mountains hiding, the people that my grandfather called our white brothers came along to where our winter supplies were. They set everything we had left on fire. It was a fearful sight. It was all we had for the winter, and it was all burnt during that night. My father took some of his men during the night to try and save some of it, but they could not; it had burnt down before we got there. Those were the last white men that came along that fall. My people talked fearfully that winter about those they called our white brothers . . . This whole band of white people [probably the Donner Party] perished in the mountains, for it was too late to cross them. We could have saved them, only my people were afraid of them. We never knew who they were, or where they came from. So, poor things, they must have suffered fearfully, for they all starved there. The snow was too deep . . . ."

42

GA1502

Sarah was sent to a Catholic mission school in California but wasn't able to stay long because the whites did not want their children going to school with Indians. For a time, she lived with a trader so she learned English. She felt that the old times were gone and that the Paiutes needed to be educated. She tried to teach her people farming and tried to convince the U.S. government to give land to each member of her tribe. She felt that whites and Indians could live together peacefully. However, some Indians felt she was doing what the whites wanted her to do, and the whites didn't trust her because she was an Indian. She was an interpreter for the U.S. government and helped settle the Bannock Uprising. She fought for the rights of her people as they were moved from Pyramid Lake, Nevada, to the Malheur Indian Reservation in Oregon, and finally to Yakima, Washington. She wrote a bill that Congress passed in 1884 that allowed the Paiutes to return and settle on their own land, but this legislation was never enforced. Even after she married a white man named Hopkins in 1882, she continued to lecture on behalf of her people, telling of the injustices that had happened to them. She died in Montana in 1891 of tuberculosis at the age of 48.

GA1502

Giving a Speech to Explain Your Beliefs Activity
Like the Speeches of Sarah Winnemucca

Sarah Winnemucca Hopkins was an interpreter and guide for the U.S. Army during the Bannock Uprising. For her bravery, she became well known and gave many speeches throughout the Eastern United States. She spoke about the injustices that had happened to her tribe. Although they were not part of the Bannock Uprising, her tribe was forced to leave their traditional lands in Nevada and were sent to Camp Harney in Oregon. Then they had to march through the snows of winter to a prison camp in Yakima, Washington Territory. Many died during this difficult march. Their lives were very hard as they lived in a livestock shed without heat and little food and had to work in the fields. Sarah was upset with the government for the way they treated her people. She met with government leaders, but they made many promises that were not kept. Sarah gave many speeches to let people know what the U.S. government had done to her people.

Give a speech about something you believe strongly about, as Sarah Winnemucca did.

1. Pick a topic that you can speak about. This needs to be a topic on which you can state your opinion. There will need to be "another side" to your belief that someone else might believe. For example, the U.S. government had a different opinion than Sarah about how to treat the Indians.

2. Write your speech on paper, planning the order carefully.

3. Practice giving the speech out loud, in private, perhaps in front of a mirror. Learn your speech so you can give it smoothly and convincingly. Time the length of the speech so it fits the correct amount of time.

4. Find an audience that would like to listen to your speech. Ask them to evaluate you so you can get better and better at delivering speeches. Have them decide if you did "fine" or "need to work on it" for each of these things:
   - Looks at the audience
   - Speaks loud enough
   - Hands held at side or uses appropriate gestures that don't detract from the speech
   - No "ums" or other "stall" words like "you know"
   - Enunciates (speaks clearly)
   - Knows information
   - Speaks on the correct topic (See #1.)

Map of Routes Across the Sierra Nevada Mountains

North

California

Nevada

Key

A = Black Rock Desert
B = Smoke Creek Desert
C = Forty Mile Desert
D = Lassen Peak
E = Pyramid Lake
F = Big Meadows (Lake Almanor)
G = Lassen's Meadows (Rye Patch Reservoir)
H = Walker Lake
I = Goose Lake
J = Lake Tahoe
K = Carson Sink/Lake Lahontan
L = Humboldt Sink
M = Humboldt River
N = Truckee Meadows (Reno)
O = Hangtown (Placerville)
P = Mormon Station (Genoa)
Q = Sutter's Fort (Sacramento)
R = San Francisco
S = Ragtown
T = Fort Churchill
U = Marysville
V = Shasta City/Fort Reading
   (Redding area)
W = Lassen's Rancho (Vina)

+ + + + + + + Applegate Route

• • • • • • • Lassen Route

○ ○ ○ ○ ○ ○ Applegate-Lassen Route

∧ ∧ ∧ ∧ ∧ Nobles Route

B B B B B Beckwourth Route

╫ ╫ ╫ ╫ ╫ Henness Route

T T T T T Truckee Route (Stevens-Donner)

J J J J J Johnson's Route

✕ • ✕ • ✕ • Mormon-Carson Route

✕✕✕ ✕✕✕ Big Trees Route

★ ★ ★ ★ ★ Sonora Route

GA1502

Truckee Route over Donner Pass
Truckee Meadows (Reno), Nevada, to Sutter's Fort (Sacramento), California

After completing the difficult Forty Mile Desert, the emigrants climbed the steep canyon of the Truckee River before arriving at Truckee Meadows. Next they faced a new challenge, crossing the high, rugged Sierra Nevada Mountains. This was also known as the Stevens-Donner route.

The Elisa Stevens party was the first group to take wagons over the Sierras. They were grateful for the assistance of Chief Truckee, a Paiute, who showed them the route to follow. In gratitude for his help, they named the river they followed the Truckee. High canyon walls made travel difficult. For example, it was necessary to cross the river ten times to progress just one mile! In some places they had to travel right up the river itself and worried that the rocks would break or overturn the wagons. The oxen hoofs became soft from being in the water so long and were worn down by the rocks. The oxen were in such pain that they wouldn't keep moving unless the drivers walked beside them in the cold, hip-deep water, urging them on. The group split, sending part ahead on horseback. They could get to Sutter's Fort more quickly and supplies could be sent back, if necessary. This group became the first whites known to have visited Lake Tahoe.

The main group with the wagons went west to what is now called Donner Lake. At this point they split again. Six wagons were left through the winter at Donner Lake, guarded by three men who agreed to stay behind. From here they could see a 1000-foot (3048-m) mountain wall, blocking the whole end of the valley. No time could be lost. The snows already buried the grass, but the oxen were saved when they found patches of tall reeds. It was a very, very difficult job getting the oxen and wagons up this steep cliff! They reached the top on November 25, 1844, which is considered the date of the true opening of the California Trail over the Sierras. They moved down the west slope of the Sierras as quickly as they could, but it was also hard going downhill. There were three to four feet (.9-1.2 m) of snow, the country was rough and unknown, and a baby had just been born. They decided to split again. Most of the cattle were butchered to be left as food, and a log cabin was built. Two men, the five wagons, and the women and children were left here. Seventeen men continued on through the snow. About a week later they arrived at Sutter's Fort and met the horseback group that had arrived a few days before. The men were not able to return to the mountain camp right away because Captain Sutter needed them to help fight the Mexicans.

GA1502

Meanwhile, the people at the camp were surprised to see two of the three men that had been left at Donner Lake. The men had become concerned at the depth of the snow and realized they wouldn't be able to hunt for food during the winter. They made snowshoes out of rawhide and the flexible hickory bows of the wagons. On the hike out, the third man, Mose Schallenberger, had been too weak to continue. He said he would return to the cabin and wait for help. It was hard to leave him, knowing he would probably die, but the two had to continue on their way. Meanwhile, some of the men in the informal "army" left Capt. Sutter. One was Dennis Martin, who knew about snowshoes and managed to get back to the camp February 20. There had been no deaths but food was so scarce they were eating animal hides. Plans were made to get the group down to the valley. Martin continued and was very surprised to find Mose alive! Mose explained that he found traps that had been left in the wagons. He had had no luck shooting animals in the snow, but he put out the traps, using parts of cow heads for bait, and was able to trap foxes to eat.

The next morning Martin and Schallenberger started over the mountains. At the same time, the women and children also moved down the mountains. Finally, on March 1, they entered the Sacramento Valley, almost exactly a year since they had left Missouri. It had been a very difficult journey, but no lives had been lost, and two babies had joined the group. The next spring the wagons were retrieved. Unfortunately, today no landmarks on this route are named for Elisha Stevens or other members of the party. They were the first to get wagons over the mountains, yet the landmarks were instead named for the ill-fated Donner Party that followed in 1846.

Once it was known that wagons could cross the mountains, more and more emigrants followed. This Truckee route, however, had been extremely difficult. The steepest part was soon abandoned by most groups for a little longer, but somewhat easier route by way of Coldstream Canyon. In 1845 Caleb Greenwood, who had been with the Stevens party in 1844, hurried east and sold his services as a guide. He avoided the steep Truckee Canyon and became the first to get his group and wagons through in one season.

GA1502

Mose Schallenberger Story
Truckee Route over Donner Pass

Mose Schallenberger was sure he would die during the winter in the Sierras as he guarded the wagons left behind by the Stevens party. When he found traps, he was able to catch food and managed to survive until he was rescued by Dennis Martin.

He dictated the experience to his daughter forty years later, ". . . to my great delight I found in one of them [trap] a starved coyote. I soon had his hide off and his flesh roasted in a Dutch oven. I ate this meat, but it was horrible. I next tried boiling him, but it did not improve the flavor. I cooked him in every possible manner my imagination, spurred by hunger, could suggest, but could not get him into a condition where he could be eaten without revolting my stomach. But for three days this was all I had to eat. On the third night I caught two foxes. I roasted one of them, and the meat, though entirely devoid of fat, was delicious. I was so hungry that I could easily have eaten a fox at two meals, but I made one last me two days. I often took my gun and tried to find something to shoot, but in vain. Once I shot a crow that seemed to have got out of his latitude and stopped on a tree near the cabin. I stewed the crow, but it was difficult for me to decide which I liked best, crow or coyote. I now gave my whole attention to trapping, having found how useless it was to hunt for game. I caught, on an average, a fox in two days, and every now and then a coyote. These last-named animals I carefully hung up under the brush shed on the north side of the cabin, but I never got hungry enough to eat one of them again. There were eleven hanging there when I came away. I never really suffered for something to eat, but was in almost continual anxiety for fear the supply would give out. For instance, as soon as one meal was finished I began to be distressed for fear I could not get another one. My only hope was that the supply of foxes would not become exhausted . . . I had just coffee enough for one cup, and that I save for Christmas . . . My life was more miserable than I can describe. The daily struggle for life and the uncertainty under which I labored were very wearing. I was always worried and anxious, not about myself alone, but in regard to the fate of those who had gone forward. I would lie awake nights and think of these things . . . Fortunately, I had a plenty of books, Dr. Townsend having brought out quite a library. I used often to read aloud, for I longed for some sound to break the oppressive stillness. For the same reason, I would talk aloud to myself. At night I built large fires and read by the light of the pine knots as late as possible, in order that I might sleep late the next morning, and thus cause the days to seem shorter. What I wanted most was enough to eat, and then next thing I tried hardest to do was to kill time. I thought the snow would never leave the ground, and the few months I had been living here seemed years. One evening, a little before sunset, about the last of February, as I was standing a short distance from my cabin, I thought I could distinguish the form of a man moving towards me. I first thought it was an Indian, but very soon I recognized the familiar face of Dennis Martin."

GA1502

Mose Schallenberger Story as a TV Interview Activity

Imagine that "talk shows" and television existed in 1845 when Mose Schallenberger was rescued. Assume you are the reporter and that you have only briefly heard his story. You have been assigned by your television station to interview him. You want the television audience to learn all the details of his winter in the Sierra Nevada Mountains. Write down the exact interview.

Example:
TV Reporter: "Mr. Schallenberger, why didn't you use your gun to hunt for food?"

M. Schallenberger: "I tried that but the snows were too deep and powdery. I couldn't move easily or quickly through them. Many of the animals had moved to lower elevations for the winter."

TV Reporter: "When hunting didn't work, what did you try next?"

M. Schallenberger: "I was guarding six of the wagons of our Stevens party. In one of them I found some traps. It gave me the idea of another way to try to catch some food."

GA1502

Beckwourth Pass–Truckee Route Alternative
Truckee Meadows (Reno), Nevada, to Marysville, California

Jim Beckwourth, a mulatto, was the son of a slave and a southern planter. For years he had traveled the West, lived among the Crow Indians, worked as a mountain man, and looked for adventure. He opened a more northerly branch of the Truckee route over the Sierras in 1851. That summer he met some emigrants at Truckee Meadows and persuaded them to try his new route. William Pickett and his family, including a ten-year-old stepdaughter, Ina Coolbrith, was part of the group. Beckwourth put the pretty little girl on the horse in front of him, and together they led the first wagon train across Beckwourth Pass. (Ina was later a friend of Mark Twain and achieved the title of Poet Laureate of California.)

Beckwourth opened the route along the Feather River to help businesses near the end of the trail at Bidwell Bar, Oroville, American Valley (Quincy), and Marysville. This was the first route to be opened especially to help the businesses in the new gold mining towns in the Sierra foothills. Beckwourth was interested in making money out of the route. He received a few hundred dollars from the merchants of Marysville to bring the emigrants through their town. He succeeded in bringing the emigrants, but unfortunately, Marysville burned down. The merchants could not pay the rest of the money they owed him. He wrote: "I was destined to disappointment, for that same night Marysville was laid in ashes. The mayor of the ruined town congratulated me upon bringing a train through. He expressed great delight at my good fortune, but regretted that their recent calamity had placed it entirely beyond his power to obtain for me any substantial reward . . . Sixteen hundred dollars I expended upon the road is forever gone . . . I can not roll a mountain into the pass and shut it up."

Beckwourth then settled just west of the pass, and made some money by trading with the emigrants. He wrote: "In the spring of 1852 I established myself in Beckwourth Valley, and finally found myself transformed into a hotel-keeper and chief of a trading-post. My house is considered the emigrant's landing-place, as it is the first ranch he arrives at in the golden state, and is the only house between this point and Salt Lake . . . When the weary, toil-worn emigrant reaches this valley, he feels himself secure . . . ."

GA1502

Advertising Your Route with a Poster
Beckwourth Pass–Truckee Route Alternative

Jim Beckwourth planned to make money out of his new Beckwourth Pass route that he opened over the Sierras. Merchants in gold mining towns at the end of the route gave him money to bring people through the mountains to their towns. He dictated his autobiography (1856): ". . . I made known my discovery [new route] to a Mr. Turner, proprietor of the American Ranch, who entered enthusiastically into my views . . . If I could but carry out my plan, and divert travel into that road, he thought I should be a made man for life. Thereupon he drew up a subscription-list, setting forth the merits of the project, and showing how the road could be made practicable to Bidwell's Bar, and thence to Marysville . . . ."

Imagine that *you* could make a lot of money if *you* could convince emigrants to take a particular trail across the Sierras to the Sacramento Valley.

1. Choose one of these routes.
   - Applegate-Lassen
   - Truckee (Stevens-Donner)
   - Mormon-Carson
   - Sonora
   - With some research you could find enough information to also choose one of these lesser-known routes: Nobles, Beckwourth, Big Trees, or Henness.

2. Draw a poster (words and pictures) that could be placed at the Humboldt Sink to convince emigrants to take your route. You will have to know enough about the route to be convincing . . . where the route goes, what difficulties they will face, natural beauties they will enjoy, why your route is best, and so forth.

The words need to be printed clearly and large enough to be read from a distance. The picture should relate to the trail. A paper frame can be glued around the poster to add to its appeal.

Donner Party Tragedy
Truckee Route (Donner Pass)

The George and Jacob Donner party was among the last to leave Independence in April 1846. There were problems all through the journey. At Alcove Springs Grandmother Keyes died. She had insisted on coming on the journey, even though she was bedridden in a wagon. Just past Fort Bridger they chose to take the Hastings Cutoff, but it was a mistake. The route had not been tried by wagons, and Lansford Hastings had gone on ahead with other wagons, so he wasn't able to lead the Donners. Hastings had said the Salt Lake Desert was forty miles (64.4 km) across, but actually it was about eighty miles (128.8 km). The desert caused great hardship. For five hot days they suffered from thirst. For five cold nights the children huddled against the dogs for warmth. They lost one-fourth of their oxen and were greatly delayed. In Nevada, James Reed got in a fight with John Snyder, a teamster. On a difficult, sandy hill, nerves had worn thin from exhaustion. They argued about whose wagon should go first. Reed told Snyder to stop his furious lashing at the tangled oxen. Snyder was killed by Reed's knife. Reed was banished and forced to travel to California alone. He left his wife, Margaret, and four children with the other wagons.

At Truckee Meadows they stopped to rest for five days, just one day too long because ten-foot (three-meter) snow drifts soon blocked their travel. Virginia Reed later wrote, "We journeyed on through the rain, looking up with fear towards the mountains, where snow was already falling although it was only the last week in October. Winter had set in a month earlier than usual! All trails and roads were covered; and our only guide was the summit which it seemed we would never reach. Despair drove many nearly frantic. Each family tried to cross the mountains but found it impossible . . . ." They were forced to stay on the east side of the Sierras, facing a winter of cold and starvation. They used Mose Schallenberger's old cabin and built other shelters, hoping to stay only until there was a break in the weather. However, the snows continued to fall and the group was stranded. To keep from starving, they reluctantly ate the flesh of those who had already died. None would eat the flesh of relatives. In one cabin, children cut up a fur rug, toasted it, and ate it. Patrick Breen kept the only diary that was written at the camp. On Christmas Day he wrote: ". . . offered our prayers to God this Cherimass morning the prospect is apalling but hope in God Amen." In February he wrote, "Mrs. Murphy said here yesterday that thought she would Commence on Milt. & eat him, it is distressing Sat 27th beautiful morning." Six times groups tried to go for help but only part of one group, with much difficulty, succeeded in reaching a rancher's house.

GA1502

When the Donners did not show up in California, James Reed realized they must still be in the mountains. A rescue mission was delayed because of the California Revolt against Mexico. Eventually, several rescue attempts brought out the survivors. When one rescue group arrived with packs of food, a woman staggered from a cabin and cried, "Are you from California or Heaven?" Reed was able to rescue his entire family. Eight-year-old Patty Reed even managed to keep her tiny doll. When many oxen had died on the Utah desert and they were forced to throw out belongings to lighten the load, Patty rescued her doll and hid it in her skirt throughout the journey.

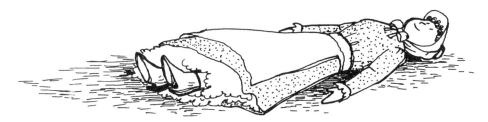

Forty of the original forty-seven had died. This was the worst disaster on the California Trail. Donner Pass, Donner Lake, and Donner Creek are names of places today that honor the memory of these emigrants. The Hastings Cutoff was used very little after this tragedy. After the Donner tragedy and until the Gold Rush, the difficult Truckee River and Donner Pass were avoided by emigrants.

Twelve-year-old Virginia Reed wrote in a letter to her cousin soon after she arrived in California, "never take no cutofs and hury along as fast as you can." The horror of the Donner experience helped later emigrants be well prepared and not delay in their travels.

"Seeing the Elephant"
Overcoming Hardship

"Seeing the elephant" was slang among the emigrants for the dangers of the trail. George Murrell wrote a letter to a friend in the East (1849): "Travel in an epidemic . . . Stand guard all night . . . And you will . . . realize what seeing the 'Elephant' means."

The saying apparently was started by a farmer. All of his life he had wanted to see an elephant. He heard that a circus was coming to town that would feature an elephant. That Saturday he loaded his horse-drawn wagon with produce he hoped to sell in town, dressed in his best clothes, and started off to "see the elephant." As he came near the town, he rounded a corner and came face to face with the elephant that was leading the circus parade. This scared his horses and they ran off, throwing the farmer and his produce from the wagon. The wagon was wrecked, his good clothes were ruined, and the horses ran away. This had been a bad experience, but he told his friends who ran to help him, "But at least I got to see the elephant."

"Seeing the elephant" became part of Western slang. Living and traveling in the West was very hard–full of tragedy, dangers, and disappointments. The story of the elephant showed the only attitude that was possible for survival. A Forty-Niner would say he was "going to see the elephant." The elephant represented the misfortunes that could happen along the way and also the wonderful sights and adventure of a lifetime. There was no shame in "seeing the elephant" because it represented something too big for their control. On the trail, when there was a difficulty, such as the death of a child, they would say they had seen the elephant. Those who turned back claimed they had seen the "elephant's tracks" or the "elephant's tail," and said that was all they cared to see!

The rugged Donner Pass presented many opportunities to "see the elephant." Wakeman Bryarly wrote (1849): "Everyone is liable to mistakes, & everyone has a right to call a road very bad until he sees a worse. My mistake was that I said I had seen "The Elephant" when getting over the first mountain. I had only seen the tail . . . I have come to the conclusion that no Elephant upon this route can be so large that another cannot be larger. If I had not seen wagon tracks marked upon the rocks I should not have known there the road was, nor could I have imagined that any wagon & team could possibly pass over in safety."

Remembering the tragedy of the Donner Party, Virginia Reed later wrote: "The misery endured during those four months at Donner Lake in our little dark cabins under the snow would make the coldest heart ache." They had definitely seen the elephant!

"Seeing the Elephant"–Overcoming Hardship Activity

Make a card showing how you have overcome "an elephant" in your life.

1. Decide upon an "elephant" (difficulty) in your life over which you had no control. Be sure this is something you wish to share with others. Examples: when you had to move to a new school, when a pet died, when you didn't get to do something you wanted to do, and so forth.

2. Fold a piece of 9" x 12" (22.86 x 30.48 cm) construction paper in half. On the outside of the card, draw a picture and write a description of what happened to you–your "elephant."

3. On the inside of the card, draw and write how you handled this difficult situation. Like the pioneers, you had no choice but to deal with the problem.

4. Display your card along with those of your friends. You will see that everyone has problems to overcome (their "elephants"), and you will learn ways to handle problems from the experiences of others.

GA1502

Mormon-Carson Route
Ragtown (West of Fallon, Nevada) to Placerville, California, and on to Sutter's Fort (Sacramento)

The Forty Mile Desert crossing on the Mormon-Carson Route (usually called the Carson Route) had no water holes. It was a relief to reach the Carson Sink where the emigrants started to follow the Carson River. At Ragtown the emigrants often paused to wash their "ragged" clothing. The river was lined with giant cottonwood trees which made the route cool and pleasant after the heat of the desert. Next they came to Mormon Station (later called Genoa) near the base of the Sierras, in the beautiful Carson River Valley. In 1851 Mormons from Salt Lake City established a trading post here in a stockaded log cabin. They sold supplies to emigrants going to California.

The Sierras seemed impossible to cross, but the emigrants found a small opening that followed the West Fork of the Carson River. Sarah Royce described the narrow canyon they climbed to Carson Pass (1849): ". . . entered the great canon. Here the road soon became so rough and steep . . . The men had hard work to drive the cattle and mules over the boulders at the frequent crossings of the stream . . . As the canon narrowed, the rocky walls towered nearly perpendicular, hundreds of feet; and seemed in some places almost to meet above our heads . . . The days were shortening fast, and, in this deep gulch, darkness began to come on early . . . ." This [8573'] pass was named for Kit Carson, the famous frontiersman, who passed through the area with John Fremont on an exploring party in 1844. He carved his name in a tree at this pass that was named for him.

Next they had a steep climb up to Emigrant Pass at 9600 feet (2926 m), the highest point on any wagon trail across the Sierras. James F. Wilkins described this climb (1849): ". . . thought advisable to feed our oxen well before we started, as we had the second summit to ascend . . . here on the very summit of the back bone of American continent, (and the backbone of the Elephant as the emigrants call it) we were favoured with a storm of hail rain and sleet . . . to add to our difficulties the lady in our company was taken with the pangs of labour, and we had to descend as quickly as possible over a most rocky road, to the first grass, which we did not reach till an hour after dark. the wagon was near upsetting several times. how she stood the jolting I cannot imagine. I now hastily pitched my tent, which I gave up for her accomadation, and before morning she was delivered of a little girl." From there it was basically downhill to the goldfields and the Sacramento Valley.

GA1502

In 1852 the Johnson's Cutoff split from the Carson Route along a more direct route to Placerville. It closely followed the route of U.S. 50 today. The Big Trees Trail opened in 1856 as another branch off the Carson Route. It came down the ridge between the Stanislaus and Moeklumne Rivers to Stockton. Businessmen from Stockton promoted the route by building eight bridges. It replaced the difficult Sonora Route to the southern goldfields. The route passed through the famous Calavaras Big Tree Grove. Jane Gould described it (1862): "Came through the most beautiful timber I ever saw. Passed the large tree called the Mother of the Forest. It is 78 feet in circumference and 360 ft. high . . . It is redwood. I thought it was as large as a tree could be but I found soon after that there was one still large . . . After getting our early supper we went to inspect the grove of world renoued large trees . . . I don't believe this grove has its equal in the world . . . At last we went to see the Big Tree. It has been cut down. It took two men 27 days. It is 29 feet in diameter. On the stump is a ballroom [dance] floor . . . Lou and I danced the schottische on it . . . ."

The Carson Route was opened through the Sierras in 1848 by members of a Mormon wagon train that was heading east, returning to Salt Lake City. They had been enlisted by the government to fight in the war against Mexico but had arrived too late. During the winter they took whatever jobs they could find and did some mining before heading back to Salt Lake City in the spring. As they crossed from west to east, they built what would become known as the Carson Route. Later in 1848 the Joseph Chiles wagon train met the Mormons along the Humboldt River. They learned of the new route over the mountains and the gold discovery. One journal from the Chiles group said the gold "really ran us all mad." The Chiles party broke some new trail and then followed the Mormon route over the Sierras. They were the first to take wagons from east to west over the Carson Route.

The Carson Route became the most popular emigrant trail over the Sierras. It was almost as direct a route to Sutter's Fort as the Truckee Route. After gold was discovered, the route had the advantage of ending right in the center of the early mining camps. It was also the easiest route over the mountains. Since the Mormons had opened it by following the ridges from the west, they had been able to pick out a fairly direct and easy route. Those that opened a route from the other direction could only start down a ridge and hope it wouldn't end abruptly in a cliff or impossible canyon. For twenty months in 1860-61, this was also the mail delivery route of the Pony Express from St. Joseph, Missouri, to Sacramento.

Writing a Pioneer or Gold Mining Song Activity
Mormon-Carson Route

California Highway 49 from Mariposa in the south to Sierraville in the north today crosses the historic gold mining region known as the Mother Lode. Many mining towns developed in these Sierra foothills in 1848-49 as gold was discovered. One of the most famous towns was Placerville. It became known as "Hangtown" because it was the first gold rush town to hang its lawbreakers. Reaching Placerville was the goal of many Forty-Niners, including Betsey and Ike in the "Sweet Betsey from Pike" song:

> *They suddenly stopped on a very high hill,*
> *With wonder looked down upon old Placerville;*
> *Ike sighed when he said, and he cast his eyes down,*
> *"Sweet Betsey, my darlin, we've got to Hangtown."*

Note: This song came West with the Forty-Niners. "Sweet Betsey" represented every girl who emigrated to California. This song is typical of the exaggerated humor that was often found in frontier songs. The tune came from England.

Write your own song about pioneer trail experiences or about life in mining camps.

1. Decide whether you will write about pioneer experiences *or* about mining camp life. Research the topic and take notes so you have plenty of accurate, interesting facts.

2. You can use a familiar tune and put your new words to it. For example, you could use the tune of "Sweet Betsey from Pike" but write your own words. Instead of using a familiar tune, you may prefer to write your own.

3. Enjoy sharing your new song with others.

GA1502

Sweet Betsey from Pike

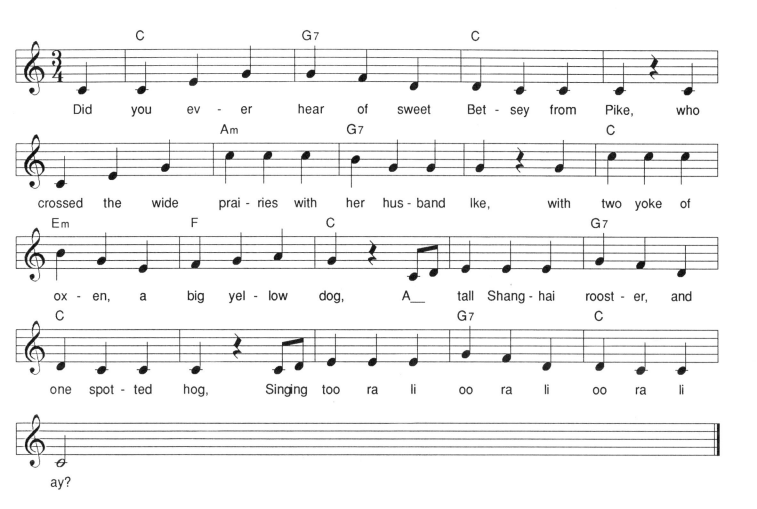

2. One evening quite early they camped on the Platte,
   Up close to the road on a green grassy flat,
   Poor Betsey, sore footed, lay down for repose,
   And Ike sat and gazed at his Pike County rose,
   Singing too ra li oo ra li oo ra li ay.

3. The Shanghai ran off and their cattle all died;
   That morning the last piece of bacon was fried;
   Poor Ike got discouraged, and Betsey got mad,
   The dog drooped his tail and looked terribly sad.
   Singing too ra li oo ra li oo ra li ay.

4. The alkali desert was burning and bare,
   And Ike cried in fear, "We're lost, I declare!
   My dear old Pike County, I'll come back to you!"
   Vowed Betsey, "You'll go by yourself if you do."
   Singing too ra li oo ra li oo ra li ay.

5. 'Twas out on the desert that Betsey gave out,
   And down in the sand she lay rolling about,
   Poor Ike, half distracted, looked down in surprise,
   Saying "Betsey, get up, you'll get sand in your eyes!"
   Singing too ra li oo ra li oo ra li ay.

6. Then Betsey got up and gazed out on the plain,
   And said she'd go back to Pike County again,
   But Ike heaved a sigh, and they fondly embraced,
   And they headed on west with his arm 'round her waist.
   Singing too ra li oo ra li oo ra li ay.

7. They suddenly stopped on a very high hill,
   With wonder looked down upon old Placerville;
   Ike sighed when he said, and he cast his eyes down,
   "Sweet Betsey, my darling, we've got to Hangtown."

GA1502

Sonora Route

Lahontan Reservoir, Nevada, to Sonora, California

The very first California wagon train, the Bidwell-Bartleson party, crossed the Sierra Mountains north of the present-day Sonora Pass in 1841. In 1852 the Clark-Skidmore party found a better Sonora route. It was still very difficult but became the emigrant route.

The Sonora Route started near today's Lahontan Reservoir where the trail left the Mormon-Carson route. Emigrant groups, starting in 1860, passed Fort Churchill. It was built to protect emigrants and new settlements in the Carson River Valley from Indian attacks.

The trail continued south to the Walker River and followed it to where the West Walker River came in through Wilson Canyon. It continued up other difficult canyons and through mountain valleys. An emigrant of 1858 wrote about Leavitt's Valley: "We descended suddenly into a large and beautiful valley . . . was one of the few truly beautiful spots in this wild region . . . a little miniature lake, the water cool and clear as crystal, and floating upon its surface was a little flock of ducks, which gave life to the picture . . . ." The trail passed Fremont Lake and crossed Emigrant Pass and Brown Bear Pass. It followed many creeks and valleys and eventually came out along the ridge between the Stanislaus River and the Tuolumne River and finally to the towns of Columbia and Sonora.

Like other routes that were promoted by businessmen, Sonora wanted emigrants to follow the route to their town. In 1853 a delegation was sent to the Carson River to find wagons that would follow the Sonora Route. The Duckwell party agreed to come but ended up facing many difficulties. At one point, a small lake blocked the way. They had to dig a ditch and lower the water level before they could continue on the trail. Wagons were smashed on the rocks. Mules and oxen died from starvation and overwork, and people almost starved too. It nearly ended with a disaster like the Donner party, but a pack train from Sonora brought them supplies at what became known as Relief Valley. When word spread of the near tragedy, most emigrants with wagons avoided this route. Later it became popular and convenient for miners with pack trains in the 1870s, after the discovery of the rich Bodie mining strike.

GA1502

Food Along the Trail
Sonora Route

The emigrants had difficult decisions to make when packing their wagons for the long journey West. They had to take wagons and animals plus the equipment and spare parts that went with them. They also had clothes, bedding, candles, water kegs, guns and ammunition, tools, medicines, ropes, equipment for cooking, materials for sewing and washing, some furniture and family treasures for their future home, and any other materials they might need for a 2000-mile (3220-km) journey. All of this had to fit in their 10' x 4' (3 x 1.2 m) wagon(s) and not be so heavy that the oxen would collapse from the strain.

In most wagons, food took up the most space. The guidebook *Brief Practical Advice* said: "Take plenty of bread stuff; this is the staff of life when everything else runs short." Two hundred pounds per adult was recommended and most was carried as flour. A lot of bacon was taken, but this term meant other types of pork as well. It was cheap meat but caused trouble because in the heat the fat melted and it turned rancid. They also took salt, sugar, coffee, and dried fruit. Canned goods were available, but they were expensive, so few were taken. The emigrants tried to get some food along the trail such as berries, bison, deer, waterfowl, and fish. Occasionally they ate "bush trout," their name for rattlesnake, plus occasionally jackrabbits and prairie dogs. Sometimes they also had to eat their cattle.

The forts that they occasionally passed had few supplies, and what was available was very expensive. When people ran low on food they tried to buy or trade for more, but sometimes they just went hungry. Some people tried to "beg." One emigrant was described in this manner: "He is accompanied by a savage-looking bull-dog, has a long rifle over the shoulder, on the end of which he carries his baggage, in a small bundle about the size of your hat. He has no provision, but gets along fairly well by sponging on his fellow travelers."

Along the Sonora route, Reuben Shaw wrote (1849): "We discovered in several localities in the mountains a kind of wild onion, which was used in flavoring soups made of bones and remnants of meat . . . also excellent as a preventative of scurvy, from which we were liable to suffer when living on an exclusive flesh diet . . . These wild up in strength. When eating them in liberal quantities, it is very doubtful whether we would have been cordially received in refined society." Emigrants knew that scurvy was caused by a lack of fresh fruits and vegetables, but they didn't know why. (Vitamin C wasn't identified as the reason until 1935.) Wilkins wrote (1849): "We are most of us taking the scurvey . . . the gums bleed and the skin is becoming discoloured in patches."

GA1502

Food Along the Trail Activity

Having a balanced diet today is as important as it was for the emigrants on their long journey. A proper diet helps the body maintain strength, work correctly, and prevent disease.

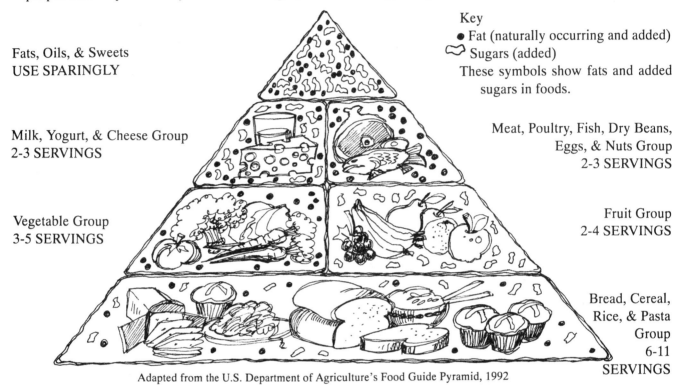

Fats, Oils, & Sweets
USE SPARINGLY

Key
● Fat (naturally occurring and added)
♋ Sugars (added)
These symbols show fats and added sugars in foods.

Milk, Yogurt, & Cheese Group
2-3 SERVINGS

Meat, Poultry, Fish, Dry Beans, Eggs, & Nuts Group
2-3 SERVINGS

Vegetable Group
3-5 SERVINGS

Fruit Group
2-4 SERVINGS

Bread, Cereal, Rice, & Pasta Group
6-11 SERVINGS

Adapted from the U.S. Department of Agriculture's Food Guide Pyramid, 1992

The U.S. Department of Agriculture and the U.S. Department of Health recommend that daily food choices are based on the following Food Guide Pyramid. This replaces the earlier recommendation of Four Basic Food Groups.

1. Plan a properly balanced meal for yourself for one day. List what you could eat for breakfast, lunch, and dinner that would give you the foods recommended by the Food Guide Pyramid. Perhaps your family would also let you try out these menus. Compare these menus with what you normally eat each day.

2. Next, plan a properly balanced meal, according to the Food Guide Pyramid, for one day for an emigrant child. Imagine that you were on the trail and you had the types of supplies typical of a pioneer wagon train. You need to prevent diseases like scurvy and have a balanced meal in order to give you strength for the difficult journey. List the foods you could eat for breakfast, lunch, and dinner.

Note: It wasn't always possible for the pioneers to have a balanced meal because of trail conditions, and they didn't always eat meals typical of what we eat today. Their large meal was often at noon. It was called "nooning" when they stopped to rest for this midday meal. Sometimes the weather didn't cooperate and made cooking difficult. Harriet Loughary felt it was easier to give up when the sand blew. She was impressed with a group of packers who knew how to cook a hot meal even with the sand: "They got their coffee and bacon all right, one held his old hat over the fire while another an old black coffee pot and a frying pan partly grease and part sand. After straining the coffee through an old dish rag, had supper all right."

Applegate-Lassen Route

Lassen's Meadows (Ryepatch Reservoir), Nevada, to Goose Lake, California

After the Donners had been trapped by heavy snows, a search was made for a lower elevation trail over the Sierras than the Truckee Route. The new choice was the Applegate-Lassen Route. It followed the Applegate Trail to northern California where the route split; the Lassen Route went south to Sacramento, and the Applegate Route went north to Oregon. The Applegate section was opened in 1846 by brothers Lindsey and Jesse Applegate. They wanted a trail that would join Oregon with the California Trail along the Humboldt River. In 1849, the Applegate-Lassen trail was heavily used by Forty-Niners and emigrants who mistakenly thought it was a shortcut to the Sacramento Valley. The emigrants didn't realize until too late that this route also included a long, difficult desert and although it was an easier crossing of the Sierras, it was 200 miles longer than the other routes.

The trail left the Humboldt at Lassen's Meadows. This difficult route wound around small mountain ranges, through stretches of desert, and followed widely scattered springs that only had small amounts of water and grass. At Rabbithole Springs there was little water or grass. Some emigrants dug deep pits to try to get more water. Kimball Webster wrote (1849): ". . . four or five wells, some 8 or 10 feet deep . . . were filled with dead animals." The cattle often tried to drink at the wells and fell in head first and drowned. The wells became choked when the carcasses swelled to tightly fit the holes with only the hindquarters and tails showing above the ground. This caused a terrible stench and spoiled the water.

The trail then led to the Black Rock Desert and across it to the Great Boiling Springs at Black Rock Point. This was another grassless, waterless 25-mile (40-km) stretch. Velina Williams wrote (1853): "The day we crossed Rabbit Hole to Black Rock we crossed a desert of pure sand, free from all kinds of vegetation, the route plainly marked by the mummyfied remains of cattle and horses that had perished of thirst and wagons abandoned because there was no teams left to draw them. All kinds of household goods thrown away to lighten loads . . . ." J. Quinn Thornton wrote (1848) ". . . we entered a country more forbidding and repulsive . . . a broad expanse of a uniform dead level plain, which conveyed to the mind the idea that it had been the muddy sandy bottom of a former lake." This area *is* part of the now dry ancient Lahontan Lake bed which also includes the Humboldt and Carson Sinks.

GA1502

(The Nobles' Road was opened as a shortcut in 1852. William Nobles took the main trail to the Black Rock Desert and then headed for Shasta City and the northern gold mining regions, by way of the Smoke Creek Desert and Lassen Peak. This was definitely the easiest route to the Sacramento Valley. It was a commercial effort to get people to Shasta City and Nobles was able to collect about $2000 for his trailblazing work.)

The Applegate-Lassen Trail continued to cross difficult land. It followed rocky ridges to the famous descent into High Rock Canyon. At the top of the hill was a brush fence the Indians used as a snare to catch jackrabbits. Delano wrote: "I came to a steep hill, down which the wagons were let with ropes into the canyon." They entered the canyon through a small, steep passage between 200-foot (61-m) reddish cliffs. Without this passage, the Applegate-Lassen Trail would not have been possible. George Keller wrote (1850): "There is a small stream of good water and grass in this valley. It is about twenty miles in length. A few miles from the ravines we found a few gallons of good vinegar, which had been left by some emigrants. This was quite an addition to the 'greens.'" Emigrants' signatures can still be seen on some canyon walls, although some have eroded and some have been vandalized.

The trail continued through dry country, over mountains, and into Surprise Valley. At this point they thought they had their first view of the Sierras, but it was actually the Warner Range. It was an extremely difficult, steep climb up Fandango Pass (6155 feet [1876 m]). The trail then dropped down into Fandango Valley which had a good supply of water and grass and was one of the best campsites along the route. Fandango Valley supposedly got its name from emigrant dances (called fandangos) held around the campfire. Since they thought they had crossed the Sierras, they celebrated by dancing. They didn't realize they still had over 200 miles (322 km) yet to travel before reaching the Sacramento Valley. Others say the name came from the dances they did to get warm. It was so cold that some emigrants apparently burned wagons for fuel.

The trail went south through Fandango Valley and along Goose Lake. At the southern end of the lake the Applegate Trail swung north towards Oregon and the Lassen section continued south to California's Sacramento Valley.

GA1502

Animal Tracks Activity
Applegate-Lassen Route

Rabbithole Springs was named by the Applegate brothers. As they were blazing the Applegate Trail, they followed rabbit tracks across the desert to find water. They felt fortunate to find water, but there was little of it for large groups of emigrants. Emigrants had to dig deep pits to try to find more water. There was also little grass, but one lady, Catherine Haun, took a creative approach to feeding her animals. Bruff observed: "Mrs Horn [Haun] gave me a slice of fried pork fat, and a cup of Coffee, so I made a very hearty meal . . . rode back . . . leaving Mrs. Horn very busy baking a number of large loaves of bread, to serve out to the horses & oxen . . . ."

Near Rabbithole Springs, the Applegate brothers followed animal tracks. It's often hard to see animals in the wild because they hide when people come near and some animals only come out at night. You can see evidence of animals, however, by learning "to read" animal tracks. You can learn "to read" the difference between the tracks of various animals.

1. Research the shapes of the tracks of different animals. On another paper, draw and label the front footprint *and* the rear footprint of each animal. Choose animals that all live in the same environment. For example, a polar bear and a jaguar don't live together, so this would not be a good choice.

   Examples:
   Black Bear   Raccoon   Beaver

2. Make stamps of the different animal tracks you drew. You can make stamps in several ways:
   a. Buy a package of Dr. Scholl's Foot and Shoe Padding. This material can easily be cut with fingernail scissors. Cut out the shape of the animal track, being careful not to lose any small pieces. Find a small block of wood for the "handle" of the stamp. Carefully peel the backing paper off the padding. The padding will be sticky. Press the "track pieces" onto the block of wood. Press the stamp into dark paint or onto an ink pad. On paper, make a print with the stamp you have made.

   b. With the help of an adult, cut a potato in half. Blot off the liquid on a paper towel. Carve the shape of an animal track using a plastic picnic knife or opened heavy paper clip. Using paint or an ink pad, make a print with your potato.

3. Using your animal track stamps, create a "scene" that tells a "picture" of what the animals have been doing. Decide what environment the animals will be in—woods, field, snowy meadow, and so forth. Draw the features of the environment, such as a pond, logs, trees, steam, open areas. Decide what each animal will be doing, such as drinking from the pond, catching food in the stream, chasing prey in a meadow, being chased to a tree. Stamp the animal tracks on the picture in a way that someone else can figure and have someone try to figure out what is happening in your scene.

This activity will help you learn how to look at tracks. For example, notice the difference between hooves and paws and whether the animal leaves claw marks or not. Look at the different patterns that are left, such as whether the hind feet land ahead of the front feet as with "bounders" like squirrels. Does the print change as the animal moves fast or slow? See if you can tell which direction an animal is moving by the direction of the paw. Notice, also, that tracks of the same animal may look different if found on snow, soil, or sand.

GA1502

Lassen Trail

Goose Lake, California, to (Lassen's Rancho)
Vina, California, in the Sacramento Valley

In 1844, Peter Lassen received a land grant, about 100 miles up the Sacramento Valley from Sutter's Fort. He wanted to lure emigrants to his ranch to bring money to the area. To get to the Lassen Trail, the emigrants had traveled the Applegate-Lassen Trail through the Black Rock Desert and over the Warner Mountains. The Applegate part of the trail turned north at Goose Lake toward Oregon. In 1848 Lassen opened a route south of Goose Lake leading toward his ranch. The route avoided the high mountain passes like Donner Pass and Carson Pass, but was much longer. The Lassen Trail generally went near today's Davis Creek, Alturas, Canby, Pit River, Big Valley, Poison Lake, Feather Lake, Susan River, Big Meadows (now Lake Almanor), Deer Creek Pass, and followed Deer Creek into the Sacramento Valley. The route was traveled most heavily in 1849.

Alonzo Delano described the area near today's Alturas, one of the many beautiful parts of the route (1849): ". . . The great valley extended many miles before us . . . a high and apparently isolated snowy peak lifted its head to the clouds . . . the clear water of the Pitt (River) was sparking in the morning sun, as it wound its way, fringed with willows, through the grassy plain. The high, snow-capped butte was Mount Shasta . . . ." The emigrants passed through beautiful areas, but many felt as P.F. Castleman: ". . . I thought there might be a beauty in those picuresque cenes . . . but after one has traveled days weeks & months in sight of such cenes there beauties become faded and are allmost entirely lost in the eye of the traveler."

For part of the route, grass and hunting were plentiful. Doyle wrote: ". . . To day I had a fine dish of soup made of a large hawk commonly called a Pine Turkey in these parts. It was very palitable; the meat was white, tender & sweet. I thought equal to any chicken I had ever eaten. All who I could persuade to taste it pronounced it excellent, and general warfare was from this time on waged against the Hawks." Some parts of the route provided little food. Doyle wrote: "Most of the day was taken up in packing our hay and in butchering of Silver, Doyle & Co's oxen for beef . . . The entire train had been out of meat for some 10 days and in fact everything else except flour & coffee." One emigrant couple had chickens. J. Goldsborough Bruff wrote (1849): ". . . an Irishman & his wife, with an ox-wagon, to the rear of which was attached a large hen-coop, full of chickens and roosters. And Pat swore by the 'howly mother of Moses,' that he'd starve before he'd kill of 'em . . . ."

Part of the Lassen Trail was very rocky and part was covered in volcanic dust. Middleton complained: ". . . fine deep dust which is reddish gets into my shoes (my boots are worn out) and helps to ruin the feet . . . If I wash my legs and feet clean, with clean socks; in one hours travel I become as dirty as ever." Other parts of the trail were marshy grasslands and some was thickly forested with spruce, pine, cedar, and oak.

Along the Lassen Trail there was fear of the Indians. Delano wrote, "About sunset, the general conversation turned upon Indians . . . when a cry was raised, 'Indians Indians! They are coming toward us!' Looking down the valley, we distinctly saw three coming up, and as they approached, we saw they were squaws. 'Get the guns, boys–shoot the Diggers,' was echoed and several jumped for their rifles. 'No, no. Don't shoot! Don't shoot squaws,' was replied. 'Let them come up; perhaps they are friendly.' Every man was on his feet . . . As they approached . . . we were at once attracted by a loud, guffatory, 'haw, haw, haw!' from Watson, and looking again, we saw that the hostile squaws were none else than his own wife and a daughter-in-law, in company with another woman belonging to his train . . . [we] recognized [our] neighbors, who had only strolled down the valley, and were now returning; but whose sun-burnt faces, soiled and dilapidated garments, had made them look more like mountain wanderers than civilized beings. No harm being done, a hearty laugh ended the horrible catastrophe."

Near the end of the trail, the landscape changed. Bruff noticed: ". . . Nearly all pine trees dissappeared all yesterday afternoon, and the crooked bunchy gnarly oaks grew so distinct and far apart . . . [like] an old orchard . . . ." The climate also changed. Middleton wrote: ". . . Have got into a mild climate now; felt no cold this morning . . . The breese feels soft this morning on your cheek like a mild warm spring breese . . . ."

At last they reached the end of the difficult trail. Doyle wrote: "We are now in the much talked of, and long looked for, Sacrmento Valey . . . At the Ranch (Lassen's Rancho) everything is a regular jam. Men going hither and yon, some in search of friends whom they are here to meet . . . some to buy provisions . . . others to get the meal without buying for they have nothing to buy with, some to pore forth curses and abuse upon Lassin for his rascally deceatfulness in making the Northern road." They were ready to start the difficult task of beginning new lives in California.

GA1502

Autumn Colors of Leaves Activity
Lassen Trail

Regardless of which route the emigrants took over the Sierra Nevada Mountains, they traveled in the fall. They had a lovely view of the changing colors of the leaves, but their main thoughts were concerns about being trapped by early snows in the mountains. Henry Austin described his view near Big Meadows on October 16, 1849: "Struck Feather River at noon. A beautiful stream of clear cold water. I sat down on a rock by its margin and admired the beautiful scenery presented to the eye.–The willows and poplars had assumed their autumnal tinge which contrasted finely with the evergreen pine and arbor vitus which grows so numerous and stately all along this river . . . water clear as crystal and rushing over a bed of long grass and pebbles . . . ."

You can see the colors of autumn in *green* leaves, *before* they change colors! Follow these steps to separate leaf pigments:

1. Think about this information: Leaves look green in the spring and summer because of the green pigment, chlorophyll. (Pigments are colored compounds found in plant tissues.) All summer the tree feeds its leaves so they can process sunlight into food (photosynthesis). In the fall, the amount of green pigment decreases. The leaves stop producing chlorophyll, and they eventually die and fall off. Even when the leaves are still green, there are other colors "hiding" in the leaves that can't be seen because of the chlorophyll. When fall colors start to show, the chlorophyll is breaking down, the "hidden" pigments begin to show up, and the leaf is dying. The color the leaf will become depends on the amount of pigment. For example, oaks, maples, and sumacs often turn brilliant shades of orange and red. Elms, birches, aspens, and poplars often turn yellow. (In some leaves, the red pigments don't exist until fall, after the chlorophyll begins to break down.)

2. You can find out if there are hidden pigments in leaves using a scientific technique called chromatography. It means "to write with color." It is a technique used for separating mixtures. Collect green leaves from trees you know will turn yellow or red in fall. Tear the leaves into tiny pieces and place them in a glass jar. Add enough acetone (nail polish remover) to the jar to cover the leaves. (**Note:** Acetone fumes should not be inhaled. Work outdoors. Don't get acetone on your skin or in your eyes. Wipe up spills so it doesn't damage the finish on furniture. It is extremely flammable. Read the warning label on the acetone, and use it only with the supervision of an adult. Be sure to use a glass jar because acetone will dissolve Styrofoam™ and some plastic!)

3. Mash the leaves into a soupy mixture with a stick that you can later throw away. Put the lid on the jar to avoid inhaling the fumes. Let the mixture stand about fifteen minutes.

69

GA1502

4. Cut a strip from a flat coffee filter (about 1½" x 3½" [3.8 x 8.9 cm]). Tape the filter strip to a pencil. Remove the jar's lid. Lay the pencil across the top of the jar. Adjust the strip so the end just touches the soupy mixture. After the liquid has gone about halfway up the strip, remove it from the liquid and lay it on a piece of paper. Observe the colors that show on the strip (probably green and yellow and perhaps some red if this is done in the fall). The acetone separated the leaf pigments from the mashed leaf mixture. When the filter paper soaked up the liquid in the jar, it also soaked up the leaf's green and yellow pigments (and maybe red), which traveled different distances up the paper. The different characteristics of the pigments caused them to stop rising at different positions on the paper.

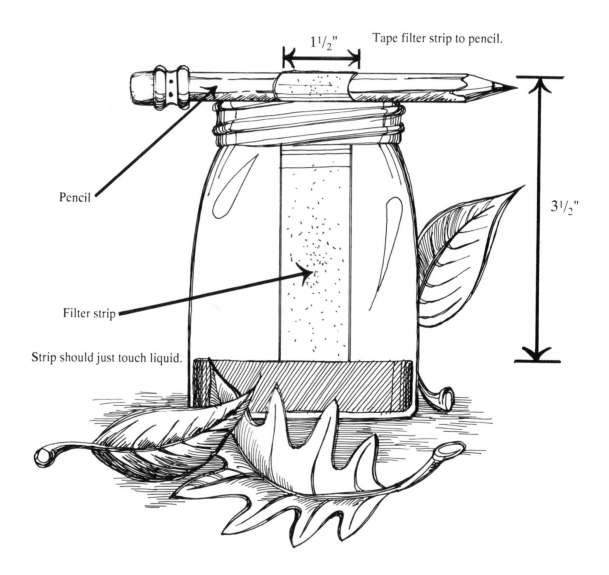

1½"

Tape filter strip to pencil.

Pencil

Filter strip

Strip should just touch liquid.

3½"

GA1502

Sailing to California Around Cape Horn
New York City, New York, to San Francisco, California

Most emigrants went to California overland, with covered wagons or using pack trains of mules. Some also took the sea route on sailing ships or steamers. The sea route was usually more expensive than traveling overland. It cost each passenger about $300, which was a lot of money in those days. During the excitement of the gold rush, scalpers often sold tickets for three times the normal price. Because of the high cost, the sea route was used by wealthier people, especially those that lived on the East Coast where it was convenient to sail from eastern ports, especially New York City. The ships followed the traditional trading route that had been used for years. The trip took between five and seven months, covered 13,000 nautical miles, and averaged 132 days.

The voyage could also be dangerous. There were often severe storms, especially around Cape Horn at the tip of South America. There was severe seasickness, and some ships sank or ran aground. Passengers often had to tie themselves to their berths during bad weather. They were constantly soaking wet. Elizabeth Gunn wrote about sailing with her four children to join her miner husband (1851): "A gale commenced on Tuesday at noon and lasted till Friday, and we were tossed about in fine order. We could neither stand nor sit and of course must lie down . . . I went to the table once, and my tumbler turned over, and rolled down and upset the salt, and cavorted against a plate, and was at last caught by the steward . . . And you can no more walk . . . than you can fly . . . ." Another danger was fire and explosions on steamers. For example, the ship *Independence* burned in 1853 and 125 out of 300 passengers died.

There were other problems on the ships. Food was considered to be very poor. Hot food was impossible during storms and water often had a foul taste. On one voyage passengers complained that "there were two bugs for every bean" with their meals, but joked that at least they had some fresh meat! Henry Huston wrote (1860) that some of the food was "old enough to vote." The lack of fresh fruits and vegetables often caused the disease, scurvy. The living quarters were very crowded, as well. Sleeping berths were often "tiered," three abreast, two feet apart, one on top of the other. The smell must have been strong, especially if people had been seasick! If ships had to wait for "fair winds," they often ran low on food and water. The ship, the *Apollo*, for example, had to wait almost two weeks west of San Francisco for a fair wind in order to sail into port.

Some emigrants found the voyage to be interesting. Most ships made one or two brief stops. When they went ashore in South America, they were able to see new and unusual sites. Mary Ann Elliott wrote from Rio de Janeiro, Argentina (1850): "I like my Voyage very much so far and anticipate a great deal of pleasure yet to come i have seen some things that i never could at home." On the Atlantic, the ports were usually Rio de Janeiro or Santa Catarina and on the Pacific, Talcahuano, or Valparaiso.

GA1502

There were advantages to the sea route. The trip could be taken during the winter months in the north which the overland pioneers could not do because they had to wait for the spring thaw. This gave the ocean travelers a head start. The sea route was extremely popular after gold was discovered in California. The Forty-Niners were eager to beat other miners, in order to get more gold. The emigrants could also carry more supplies on a ship than they could in a covered wagon.

When they arrived in San Francisco, the Forty-Niners quickly left the ships and headed for the goldfields. Often, the ships' crews also decided to become miners. The San Francisco harbor became jammed with ships that were abandoned and left to rot!

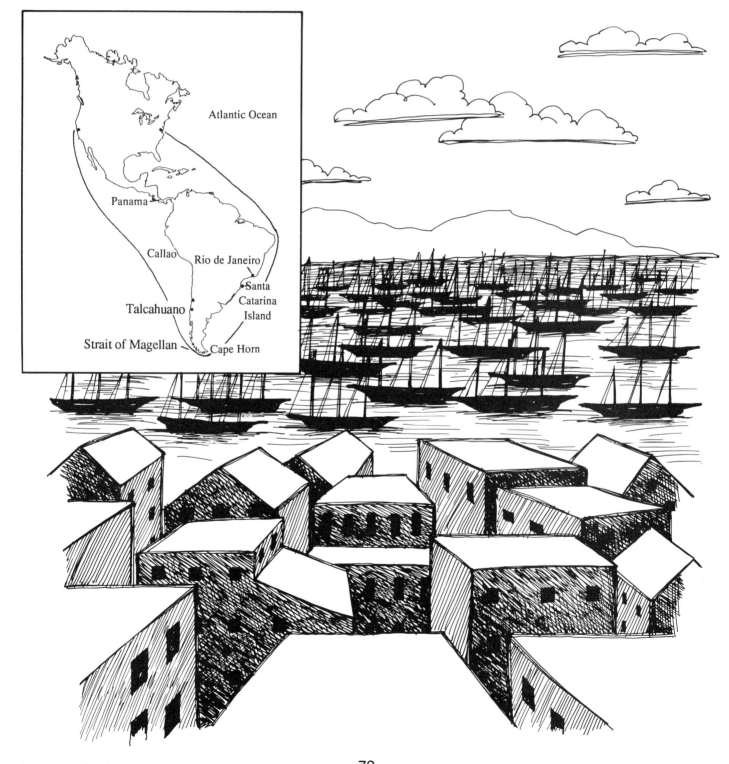

GA1502

Choosing Favorite Books Activity
Sailing to California Around Cape Horn

The long voyage from the East Coast of the United States to California was often boring. There was little change of scenery, and each day was spent much like the day before. One passenger described how he passed the time: "Today I opened my big box and spread all its contents and then stowing it away again. One man came below and seeing me thus engaged, proceeded to unpack *his* trunk. We both agreed it was a pointless proceeding, yet the time passed pleasantly." Another man spent much of his time reading, playing euchre [a card game], hunting lice, and carving canes and rings. He also played jackstraws. This was a game played with narrow strips of wood or bone. The strips were tossed into a jumbled heap, and players tried to remove them one at a time without moving any of the others.

Some people came well-prepared for the long voyage. One man brought a 150-volume library. It was probably read so many times by the travelers that there wasn't much left of it when they reached California. Books were also popular on the wagon trains. Charles Gray wrote (1849): ". . . I had borrowed a copy of Shakespeare of Mrs Berry & need hardly say it was worth its weight in gold to me, reading it in the wagon when the road was good. I read it nearly through & found it as I have for the 100'th time, a most Delicious treat . . . ."

Imagine you were traveling to California, either by the ocean route or the land route, and could take just five books with you because of limited space. Tell what those books would be.

1. Name the books. Remember to capitalize the main words, underline the titles, and don't put quotation marks around the titles. Also name the authors of the books.

2. Write a summary of what each book is about.

3. Tell why you would choose to have each book with you on the long journey.

4. If you know how to write a bibliography, write one for each of the five titles. There are several acceptable styles of bibliographies, but one is shown here as an example:

   Groh, George W. *Gold Fever*. New York: William Morrow & Co., 1966.

Crossing Central America

From the East Coast of the U.S., Across Panama, Nicaragua, or Mexico and up the West Coast to California

Crossing the Isthmus of Panama was difficult but was the shortest route to California. There were three parts to the Isthmus route. Emigrants sailed from the East Coast of the United States to Panama's Atlantic Ocean side. Then they crossed the Isthmus by canoe and mule (and by 1855, by railroad). They then took a ship from Panama's Pacific side to San Francisco, California.

After the voyage from the United States, the passengers were let off at Chagres, a small village. Panama was quite a shock to the emigrants. The primitive hotels were just bamboo huts. Mary Ballou wrote home about the "hotel" (1851): ". . . no floor but the ground for my bed . . . I wept biterly . . . Laid on the ground. the monkies were howling the Nighthawks were singing the Natives were watching." They could get a meal of stewed monkey or iguana.

The emigrants had to figure out how to get across the Isthmus. The journey started at the Chagres River. They could travel aboard dugout canoes, called bungoes, which were made from 15-25' (4.5-7.6 m) single mahogany logs that the natives poled upriver. They also had a choice of starting the first eight miles (12.8 km) on overcrowded steamboats and then switching to the bungoes. Many emigrants enjoyed the canoe ride. Lucilla Brown wrote that she found the beautiful scenery "full of exciting interest" and the jungle full of "flowers, birds of gay plumage flying hither and thither, the chattering of monkeys, the scream of parrots . . . I am perfectly delighted."

The most dangerous part of the Isthmus trip was after the villages of Gorgona and Cruces where they left the canoes. They had to travel on foot or mule in a hot, humid climate. Some men even hired natives to carry their wives and young children in hammocks! Jennie Megquier wrote (1849): ". . . one of the roughest roads in the world, nothing but a path wide enough for the feet of the mule, which if he should make a misstep you would go to parts unknown . . . ." Women were often encouraged to wear men's clothing and to ride astride the mule like a man, rather than side-saddle like "proper women" did in those days. One woman wrote that there was "great frolicking and laughing with the ladies while fixing away on the mules . . . I shall never forget *my* feelings when I found myself seated astride my mule, arrayed in boots and pants . . . ."

When they reached the Pacific Ocean at Panama City, they tried to find a ship to take them to San Francisco. There were often many people waiting and prices were high. There were no wharves in Panama City so the ships were anchored out in the harbor. People had to wade to row boats, and then the row boats took them out to the ships where they were lifted aboard. This loading procedure upset many of the "proper ladies." Many emigrants had to camp for months in the hills of Panama City or rent rooms in primitive, dirty hotels. During their delay, some emigrants went sightseeing. The Megquiers, for example, had many adventures as they visited the island of Taboga. They slept in hammocks, killed scorpions, had to have natives dig jiggers (chiggers–mites) out of their toes, and saw a 9-foot (2.7-m) snake shot out of a mango grove!

The completion of the Panama Railway shortened the time of the Isthmus crossing. When Mallie Stafford crossed on the railroad, she described it as crowded with about 900 passengers: "There was the Frenchwoman, with her poodle; . . . the old maid, with her bird-cage; the Dutch woman, with her four children, *and* her pair of twins in her arms . . . ."

GA1502

By 1853 approximately 3000 emigrants a month crossed Central America via Nicaragua. It was also a rough crossing but was easier than Panama. From the Atlantic side small steamboats carried passengers about 75 miles (120 km) up the San Juan River to Lake Nicaragua. Larger steamboats crossed the lake, about another 75 miles (120 km). From there they rode mules the last 13 miles (21 km) to the Pacific. This was twice the distance of the Panama crossing, but the mule ride was shorter and less dangerous. An emigrant lady who crossed in 1852 explained that it was dusk by the time they crossed Lake Nicaragua and had to begin the mule ride. She wrote: "The forest [jungle] became dark, the trail more uneven, sometimes steep up and sometimes steep down. In the forest there appeared almost as many stars as in the heavens, because all about there were numerous fireflies. The humming of insects and the calling of the monkeys, although loud enough, were sometimes lost in the yelping of wolves. Even a tiger was heard." (The tiger was probably a jaguar.) Jennie Megquier wrote from Nicaragua on a second trip to California (1855): "We spent three days very pleasantly although all were nearly starved for the want of wholesome food but you know my stomach is not lined with pink satin, the bristles on the pork, the weavels in the rice and worms in the bread did not start me at all, but grew fat upon it all . . . had a small room with scarce light enough to see the rats and spiders . . . ."

Diseases from Mosquitoes
Crossing Central America

Mary Crocker complained about everything on her crossing of Nicaragua. The boats were "old & oh so dirty" and the weather so "*hot*, we could hardly breathe." She said: "the water was *dreadful poor* too. I did not have a good drink from the time I left N.Y. until we reached San Francisco, nor did I relish a single meal . . . The water . . . We called it "Alligator Soup . . . ."" She also complained about the insects: "The mosquitoes and flies and bugs biting all the time. Some of the ladies looked as if they had the smallpox or some kind of spotted distemper."

Emigrants were surrounded by unhealthy conditions while crossing Panama and Nicaragua. The food and water were often unsanitary; being injured in an accident was common, and there was a danger of being bitten by disease-carrying mosquitoes.

To most people in the United States today, the mosquito is just a pest. Its bites cause itching because of an allergic reaction people have to the mosquito's saliva. The body reacts by sending extra blood to the bite which causes it to swell. Mosquitoes don't bite because they are hungry. Both males and females eat nectar from flowers and juices from plants. Females "bite," or rather suck blood from under human skin, to get protein for their eggs. Mosquitoes are attracted to their prey mainly by carbon dioxide, the ashes of burned oxygen and sugar which are exhaled with every breath. Mosquitoes are also attracted to large, dark silhouettes and usually bite the first large breathing silhouette that they encounter.

Mosquitoes spread the diseases of yellow fever, malaria, and encephalitis. (In 1904, work on the Panama Canal was halted because yellow fever had killed so many workers.) Research information about the diseases that mosquitoes spread. Fill out the information on the chart on page 77.

Diseases from Mosquitoes Activity

Mosquitoes spread the diseases of yellow fever, malaria, and encephalitis. (In 1904, work on the Panama Canal was halted because yellow fever had killed so many workers.) Research information about the diseases that mosquitoes spread. Fill out the information on this chart.

	Yellow Fever	Malaria	Encephalitis
What type of mosquito causes the disease?			
What are the symptoms of the disease?			
How is the disease treated?			
How long does it take to get over the disease?			

You might also want to find out *good* things that mosquitoes do for the world too.

Draw and color a scientific (accurate, detailed) picture of a mosquito. Label it with the name of the type of mosquito you drew.

GA1502

Map of the California Gold Country

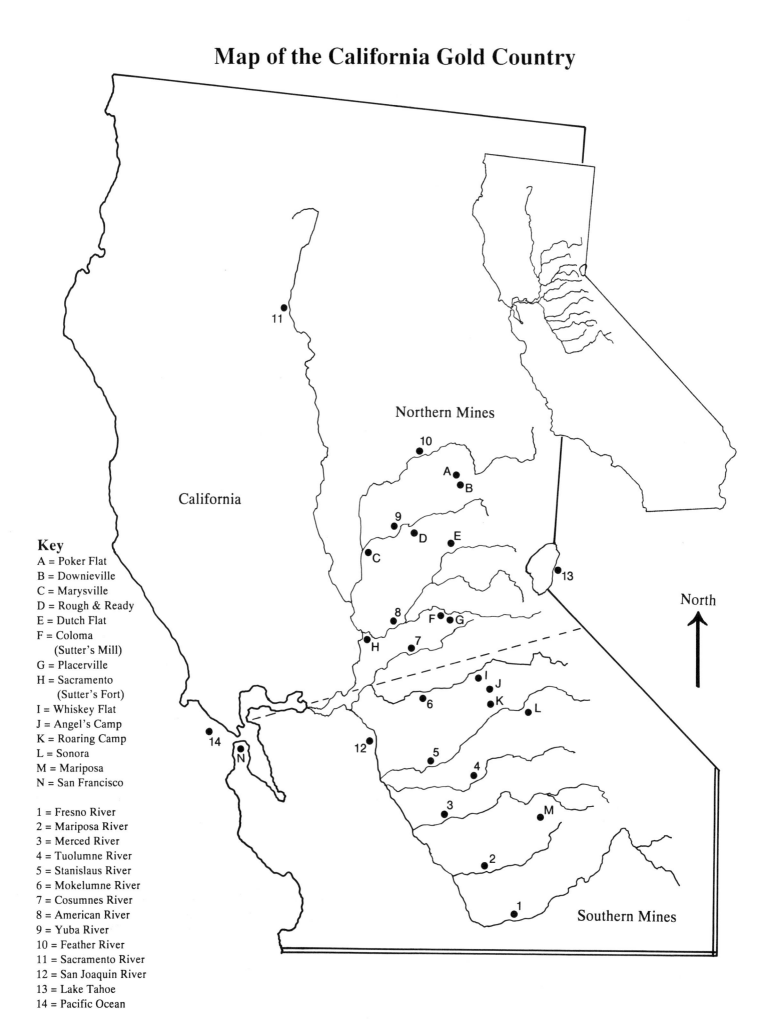

Northern Mines

California

Key
A = Poker Flat
B = Downieville
C = Marysville
D = Rough & Ready
E = Dutch Flat
F = Coloma
   (Sutter's Mill)
G = Placerville
H = Sacramento
   (Sutter's Fort)
I = Whiskey Flat
J = Angel's Camp
K = Roaring Camp
L = Sonora
M = Mariposa
N = San Francisco

1 = Fresno River
2 = Mariposa River
3 = Merced River
4 = Tuolumne River
5 = Stanislaus River
6 = Mokelumne River
7 = Cosumnes River
8 = American River
9 = Yuba River
10 = Feather River
11 = Sacramento River
12 = San Joaquin River
13 = Lake Tahoe
14 = Pacific Ocean

North

Southern Mines

78

John A. Sutter and James W. Marshall
The Discovery of Gold in California

Sutter had come to California from Switzerland to build an agricultural empire with pastures, vineyards, mills, and villages of workshops and stores. He was helped in his work by Indians, Mexicans, Europeans, and some American emigrants. By the end of 1847 he was reaching his goal. He even had about 150 Mormons who had come to California as soldiers in the Mexican War and would not be returning to Salt Lake until the next spring. With this unexpected labor, he set to work building a flour mill and a sawmill.

The water-powered sawmill was being built about 45 miles (72 km) up the American River from Sutter's Fort in the Coloma Valley. James Marshall was supervising the building of this mill. Marshall was considered a loner and rather peculiar, but he was a good carpenter. Marshall and his men built the frame and dam for the mill, installed iron machinery, and dug a 150-yard (136-m) long tailrace ditch to channel water from the river to the wheel.

On January 24, 1848, Marshall inspected the lower end of the tailrace to check its depth. He was surprised to find what he thought was gold and reported it to the other men. They thought it was another one of his strange thoughts and ignored him. Only one man thought it was worth noting in his diary. Henry Bigler wrote: "This day some kind of mettle was found in the tail race that looks like goald." The next day Marshall blocked the tailrace and found more gold. The men were skeptical at first but tried pounding it and biting it, and it wouldn't break. Jennie Wimmer, the camp cook and laundress and only woman in camp, dropped a piece of the metal into a kettle of soap she was boiling to see if lye would corrode it. She said: ". . . A plank was brought for me to lay my soap onto, and I cut it in chunks . . . there was my gold as bright as could be."

The gold discovery was kept a secret at first. Astonishingly, the men agreed to finish building the mill and Marshall would give them time off afterwards to prospect. On the 27th, Marshall rode to Sutter's Fort to show Sutter the gold. They did further tests on the metal and realized what the discovery meant. They were worried about the mills not being completed and the work crews leaving if they knew about the gold. The two men agreed to keep it a secret, even from Sutter's journal. He only wrote: "Mr. Marshall arrived from the Mountains on very important business." The gold could either help Sutter's empire or destroy it. Through his charm, hospitality, and generosity, he had befriended the Mexican rulers who had granted him the land in 1839 and the Americans who now ruled California. Sutter was forty-four years old and had a wife and four children back in Switzerland. However, he had invented a more noble past and claimed to be Captain Sutter from the Royal Swiss Guards of King Charles X of France. Sutter visited the mill to see the gold for himself and brought gifts of pocketknives for the men.

Sutter and Marshall then worked out a plan. They drew up an agreement with the local Yalesumni Indians to get legal title to the gold for about 12 square miles (19 sq. km). The agreement didn't mention gold directly but gave Sutter the right to the land for timber cutting, road building, erecting the mill, farming, and the right to "open such Mines and work the Same as the aforsaid tract of land May Contain." In return, the Indians would receive $150 a year in tools and clothes. The chiefs signed the documents with their X marks. The lease was meaningless without the approval of Governor Richard Mason, governor of the military government of California. Mason denied Sutter's lease, saying the U.S. did not recognize the right of Indians to sell or lease land. This gave Sutter no power when many prospectors moved onto his property to mine for gold.

GA1502

Meanwhile, Sutter had asked the mill workers to tell no one for six weeks, the time needed to finish the sawmill. Several of the men, including Sutter, couldn't contain their secret and told friends of the discovery. Gradually, Sutter's workers left for the hills. He wrote: "Everybody left me from the Clerk to the Cook. I began to harvest my wheat, while others was digging and washing Gold . . . ." On March 11 Marshall and the Mormon crew finished the sawmill as they promised and were free to prospect. (Within four years, Sutter was bankrupt. He spent many years unsuccessfully trying to get a clear title to his property and compensation for his loss.)

By March, the word of gold had spread by word of mouth to San Francisco and on the 15th a notice was in the newspaper. It wasn't until May, however, that the skepticism was gone and the people of San Francisco left for the Gold Country. The male population of San Francisco on May 12, 1848, was approximately 600. On May 15 it was perhaps 200! John Sutter felt that May 19, 1848, was the day "the great rush from San Francisco arrived at the fort . . . All was in Confusion . . . all left their wives and families in San Francisco, and those which had none locked their doors, abandoned their houses, offered them for sale cheap . . . Some of these men were just like crazy."

The first main communication to reach the rest of the U.S. came in the summer. On August 2 Kit Carson arrived in Washington, D.C., with letters and a copy of the April 15 edition of the *California Star*, the first newspaper to tell of the gold discovery. Word of the gold discovery was printed in several newspapers, but people were skeptical and reports were thought to be exaggerated. Exactly ten months after James Marshall found the first gold, the New York *Herald* marked November 24, 1848, as the day "California gold fever broke out in New York." Word spread throughout the East Coast. On December 5, President Polk delivered a message to Congress: ". . . The accounts of the abundance of gold in that territory are of such an extraordinary character as would scarcely command belief were they not corroborated by the authentic reports of officers in the public service . . . ." Samples of the gold were put on display in the War Department. One reporter wrote about having no doubt that it was real gold and not mica: "Any goose who could talk to 'mica' after seeing these specimens would not be worth noticing; it is no more like mica than it is like cheese."

GA1502

The rush was on! As people left by ship to California, they often made up words to the popular song "Oh, Susannah" such as these verses that were sung as the ship *Eliza* set off for California from Salem, Massachusetts:

I'm going to California-i-a, the gold dust for to see.
It rained all night the day I left, the weather it was dry.
The sun so hot I froze to death–Oh brothers, don't you cry!
Oh, California, that's the land for me.
I'm going to Sacramento with my washbowl on my knee.

I thought of all the pleasant times we've had together here,
I thought I ort to cry a bit, but couldn't find a tear.
The pilot bread was in my mouth, the gold dust in my eye.
And though I'm going far away, dear brothers, don't you cry!
Oh, California, that's the land for me,
I'm going to Sacramento with my washbowl on my knee.

I soon shall be in Francisco, and then I'll look all 'round,
And when I see the gold lumps there I'll pick them off the ground.
I'll scrape the mountains clean, my boys, I'll drain the rivers dry,
A pocket full of rocks bring home, so brothers, don't you cry!
Oh, California, that's the land for me,
I'm going to Sacramento with my washbowl on my knee.

GA1502

Newspapers Reported the Discovery of Gold Activity
John A. Sutter and James W. Marshall

Sam Brannan was an important leader and businessman in early-day San Francisco. Among his many businesses, he founded the *California Star* newspaper, printing it on a press he had brought from the East. The other newspaper in San Francisco at the time was the *Californian*. Although Sutter and Marshall tried to keep the January 24, 1848, discovery of gold a secret, the news soon spread around the world. It first appeared in a newspaper on March 15. The story was on the last page of the four-page *Californian* and was only one paragraph long. The article read:

Gold Mine Found
In the newly made raceway of the Saw Mill recently erected by Captain Sutter, on the American Fork, gold has been found in considerable quantities. One person brought thirty dollars worth to New Helvetia [Sutter's Fort], gathered there in a short time. California, no doubt, is rich in mineral wealth; great chances here for scientific capitalists. Gold has been found in almost every part of the country.

The last sentence was hardly true, but the rest was accurate. Three days later the *California Star* carried a similarly low-key story. It used more space to report a coal discovery that turned out not to be true. The people of San Francisco were very skeptical. By May 29, however, so many people believed the stories that they had left the city to mine for gold. The *Californian* had to shut down because there were few readers left. Its last issue said: "The whole country resounds with the sordid cry of 'gold! Gold!! GOLD!!!' while the field is left half planted, the house half built, and everything neglected but the manufacture of shovels and pickaxes." This article had the first published mention of the phrase that would be used to describe the mining: in "the rush for gold" it was every man for himself. Two weeks later the *California Star* also closed. It ended with "Let our word of parting be, Hasta luego." The editor, Edward Kemble, also left for the mines.

Imagine you are a reporter for a newspaper at the time of the California Gold Rush. Choose *one event* in gold rush history and report on it for your newspaper. For that one event, write a news story that would be appropriate for the front page, a cartoon (entertaining or editorial), an editorial, and a want ad.

You are not limited to these, but here are some possible topics: Marshall's discovery of gold, life at Sutter's Fort, the sea voyage around Cape Horn, the trip across the Isthmus of Panama, life in San Francisco, life in a mining camp, life for the minorities, life for a woman, life for a child.

GA1502

Mining for Gold in California

California's "Gold Country" is found in the foothills between the Central Valley and the peaks of the Sierra Nevada Mountains. Rivers flow through this region with Indian names like Tuolumne and Mokelumne; Spanish names like Calaveras and Mariposa; and American names like Bear, Feather, and American. Through these foothills, between 2000' to 5000' (609 to 1524 m) elevation, was a large vein of gold 120 miles (193 km) long, stretching from Coloma in the north to Mariposa in the south. The vein was known as the Mother Lode to the miners.

The tremendous movement of the earth's crust that pushed up the Sierras, creating these great mountains, was also responsible for the gold and other metals. When underground volcanic magma (molten rock) pushed the granite to the surface, the gold was found in long, narrow veins which were originally cracks in the rocks. Winter after winter of geologic time, rain and snow eroded the mountains. Eventually, huge chunks of rock fell off the mountains, breaking into boulders, then into pebbles, into flakes, and then dust. Season after season the particles of gold washed downstream. Since gold is heavy, it often fell into cracks in the rocks or settled into deep holes in the riverbed. The Spanish word *placer* referred to gold in its loose or eroded state as opposed to gold still in veins.

Few prospectors knew geology but soon learned the best places to look for gold. The richest placers were found where swift streams slowed down as they flowed onto more level terrain. The sand and gravel often contained other yellowish or glittering minerals, such as iron pyrites (fool's gold) or mica, which could confuse new miners. Gold was unmistakable to people who had bit it between their teeth. It was soft and wouldn't break under pressure. It would not rust or tarnish, even after lying for centuries in the water.

In 1848, except in the making of false teeth, gold was relatively useless compared to iron, tin, and copper. However, it was rare, beautiful, easy to make into jewelry because it was soft, and could be a display of wealth so people "rushed" from all over the world to try to get rich from the streams and mountains of California. The gold rush couldn't have been timed better because the national economy was depressed since the end of the Mexican War and the country needed gold.

When miners first "worked" a placer, they were able to mine with just a shovel and a washing pan made of tin or iron. The pan measured about 10" to 15" (25 to 38 cm) across and 3" to 4" (7 to 10 cm) deep. If they didn't have pans, they often used Indian willow baskets or Mexican wooden bowls. The miner first filled the pan with gravel and then swirled it around underwater. With small jerks it was lowered in and out of the water to wash out lighter sand, leaving only the heavier gold. The pan was versatile and could also be used to wash clothing, feed a mule, or fry bacon! It wasn't hard to pan for gold, but it meant hours of squatting in ice-cold water, rotating the pan until the person's arms were numb. Miners tried to make the job easier by inventing other tools for separating out the gold, such as the cradle (or rocker), the long tom, and the sluice, but they were all hard work.

GA1502

The size of a mining claim was determined mainly by the richness of the area. In rich areas it could be as small as 100 square feet (9 sq. m) and as much as 10,000 square feet (900 sq. m) at the poorer sites. Each miner was allowed one claim. To stake a claim, miners simply picked their land, pounded wooden stakes at the corners, posted a sign, and recorded the claim with a camp recorder. They could keep the claim as long as they continually worked the site which generally meant it had to be worked one day out of three. After ten days someone else could claim an unworked site. Even though a site might include part of a river, no one could ever dam a river because all miners had rights to the water. Disputes were settled by juries of other miners. Newcomers often complained that it was hard to find unclaimed land.

As miners discovered how difficult it was to get the gold, some became discouraged. Hiram Pierce wrote: "The Senery at the river [American River] is wild in the extreme . . . Prices high . . . At night the Wolves and Kiotas give us plenty of music. I would gladly warn my brethren & friends against comeing to this place of Torment. Verry much fatigued, my back getting lame in consequence of getting my feet wet & sleeping on the ground nights. A great many are laid up about us, some with sore hands & feet caused by poison & some with disentary." These reports of hardships didn't stop "Gold Fever" and people continued to come.

Although most gold was found by hard work, there are many bizarre, wild stories of how people discovered gold. For example, three Frenchmen uprooted a tree stump from the middle of the Coloma road and dug $5000 in gold from the hole! A man who had been sitting on a rock, feeling discouraged and homesick, stood and angrily kicked the rock. The rock rolled away, exposing a gold nugget! In another case, a miner's mule was staked out for the night. When the stake was pulled up in the morning, gold was found in the hole!

Many women were miners too. One woman took her "crevicing spoon" out among the rocks and searched for gold each day after she finished her housework. In one year she mined $500. Elizabeth Gunn from Sonora wrote (1851) that a "Frenchman and his wife live in the nearest tent, and they dig gold together. She dresses exactly like her husband–red shirt and pants and hat." Some women earned more money than the men who were mining by cooking, sewing, cleaning, ironing, washing, dancing, and pouring drinks. Men would pay well for women's cooking. "Aunt Maria" was a former slave freed in California who earned $100 a week cooking for the Gunn family. She also managed her own boarding house and made a lot of money cooking for weddings and banquets.

84

GA1502

In 1849, of the 85,000 men who came to the goldfields, about 23,000 were not U.S. citizens. The mining camps were not tolerant places and there was much discrimination against people from other countries, as well as American Indians. Americans did not want to share their gold and towns with foreigners such as the British, Australians, Germans, Frenchmen, Latin Americans, or Chinese. For example, thousands of Chinese came to mine even though they were mistreated. They were allowed to mine only where the whites had already mined or where no one else wanted to mine. They were often beaten, run out of town, and had their homes and businesses destroyed. The Indians saw their land destroyed, their streams polluted, and game scared away. Frustration over hard work and smaller profits as more and more miners came caused prejudices to become more intense. Foreigners were not protected by the miners' system of justice. Punishments included hanging, beating, banishment from the camp, jail, or fines. A murder a day became common. In 1850 the California Legislature started taxing foreign miners, so many left, but the prejudice remained for years.

A branch office of the U.S. Mint was built in San Francisco. Wise miners took their bags of gold dust to be weighed and sold at the mint. The official rate was $16 per ounce, instead of the market price that varied from place to place and could sink to $8. At the mint, the gold dust was melted, refined, and cast into strips and then punched into coins. The coins were pressed and stamped into legal money with Liberty heads on the faces and eagles or wreaths on the backs. During its first year, the mint produced $4 million in gold coins and by 1856, it produced nearly $24 million, including silver as well. There was also corruption at the mint. A janitor who was praised for ridding the building of rats was finally found to be sewing $20 gold pieces inside each dead rat before throwing it on the trash heap. He returned after work, collected the rats, slit them open, and took the money!

85

After a few years of finding surface gold quite easily, more sophisticated engineering and equipment was needed to get the gold. Mining changed from an adventure to an industry. By the mid-1850s, large-scale mechanized mining companies had replaced many of the individual prospectors. Machines tore up the landscape to expose streambeds. Entire river courses were moved by systems of dams and flumes. To get ore that was buried in quartz deposits deep in the earth, shafts were driven down as deep as 700 feet (213 m). Huge hoisting wheels raised the soil and rock to the surface. Hydraulic mining caused the most damage to the land. For example, at the Malakoff Mine, streams of water daily tore off 50,000 tons (45,000 tonnes) of gravel from the mountains, and left a 550-foot-(167-m-) deep canyon.

Most Forty-Niners dreamed of making their fortunes and then returning home to the East with their wealth. This usually didn't happen. Most only found enough gold to keep themselves alive. Some of them sang, "Farewell, Old California, I'm going far away, Where gold is found more plenty, in larger lumps they say," and left for new mines in Australia, British Columbia, Oregon, Idaho, Montana, Nevada, Colorado, or for the Black Hills of Dakota Territory. Others settled down in California and started new jobs such as storekeepers, farmers, hotel keepers, or loggers. Others returned to the East, with or without their fortunes. Franklin Buck was persuaded to stay and settle in the Napa Valley with his wife. He wrote to his sister in the East: "It will be a humdrum slow business picking grapes and milking cows and raising chickens. But on the other hand we are getting along in life and we had better take a certainty of having a good living than the uncertainty of making money. I have given up the idea of ever finding a rich mine or making a fortune . . . I don't know where you can find such a beautiful climate and valley, cloudless skies, warm as May, the hills and valley all green. Wheat is about two inches high; the almond trees just ready to burst into bloom. Roses and lilacs are leafing out. I am adept at making butter. It is gilt edged, yellow as gold."

Mohs' Test for the Hardness of a Rock Activity
Mining for Gold in California

The solid part of the earth is made of rocks. Rocks are made of minerals found in the earth's crust. The crust has over 2000 different minerals but only about fifty are commonly found. All metals that we use come from the crust. A mineral that contains a metal is called an ore. Copper, iron, and lead are metals. Aluminum is the most common metal. Gold and silver are metals that are popular for jewelry, ornaments, and coins. Gold is also used for filling teeth, and silver is used in making film. Several tests are used by geologists to identify minerals: color, luster (the way light reflects), streak (colored streaks when rubbed), texture, hardness, magnet test, cleavage (splitting of mineral into pieces), and chemical tests.

The Mohs' Scale of Hardness classifies minerals according to their relative hardness. It can be used for mineral identification but not for rock identification since most rocks are made of several minerals, each of which may be a different hardness. Friedrich Mohs (pronounced Moze) was a German mineralogist who introduced the scale of mineral hardness in 1812. Minerals vary in hardness, so if a mineral of unknown hardness is scratched by a mineral of known hardness then the unknown hardness must be lower. The higher the number, the harder the mineral.

Practice the Mohs' Scale of Hardness on rocks. Doing the test on a mineral collection works better, but using rocks will give the idea of how minerals are tested for hardness. The Mohs' scale gives minerals a score for hardness. For this activity, the scale of hardness from 1-7 will be used. (Examples of minerals with greater hardness: 8–topaz, 9–corundum, 10–diamond) Test at least three rocks. Place a small piece of adhesive tape on each rock. Label each rock A, B, or C. Start answering questions from the top of the chart for each rock. When you come to the first "yes" answer, write that score (of hardness) on the rock. (Have an adult help with the knife tests.)

Mohs' Test Question	Yes or No	Score	Example
Will the rock fall apart in your hands?	_____	1	Talc (softest)
Will your fingernail scratch it?	_____	2	Gypsum
Will a penny scratch it?	_____	3	Calcite
Will a knife scratch it if you press gently?	_____	4	Fluorite
Will a knife scratch if you press hard?	_____	5	Apatite
Will the rock scratch a knife blade?	_____	6	Orthoclase
Will the rock scratch a mirror?	_____	7	Quartz

Life in California During the Gold Rush

San Francisco was a fast-growing, wild town in 1849. Ships from around the world unloaded Forty-Niners. When they first arrived, many stayed on a nearby beach called Happy Valley in tents or even in packing boxes, waiting to learn how to find the goldfields. They learned that Sacramento was the town that served the northern mining regions and Tuleburg (later named Stockton) was the supply and departure point for the mines in the south.

The land near where the America River flowed into the Sacramento River would become Sacramento, California's capital city. At the end of 1848 there were no houses there, but with the arrival of so many gold miners, sales of lots reached a frenzy in early 1849, and by the end of the year, the town had 12,000 people! Even more people camped outside of town in tents and wagons. Emigrants that came overland arrived at the mining camps as they descended the Sierras. Those who came by ship had to travel upriver from San Francisco by boat. Most then made deals to have their gear carried the rest of the way by wagon or mule train while they walked over the difficult trails. The route was muddy and cold in the winter and very hot and dry in the summer. The months on the ship had left most people in poor physical condition for the long hike to the mining camps. The mining camps (small "towns") throughout the foothills of the Sierras often had colorful names such as Angels Camp, Coyote Diggings, Old Dry Diggings, Drunkards Bar, Slumgullion Gulch, Murderers Bar, Mad Mule Gulch, Rattlesnake Bar, Dead Man's Bar, and Whiskytown.

Most towns followed the same pattern of rapid growth (and often decline). A miner would find a big strike of gold. Others would hear of the gold and would move to that stream. A small community would be formed and a store would be built. Within a year there would usually be a blacksmith, pharmacy, bank, church, newspaper, fire department, and mail would begin to arrive. Prices were high. For example, miner Edward Buffum's bill for breakfast groceries totalled $43 for sardines, hard bread, butter, cheese, and ale. If gold ran out or there was news of better gold somewhere else, the town was abandoned and would develop in the new location.

Women were a rare sight in mining camps, but they arrived when towns began to grow. (In 1850 just under 8 percent of California's population was female.) Single women found it easy to find a husband and widows didn't stay single for long. Peter Decker wrote (1851): "Mr. Apperson was married to Mrs. Brondurant. He is a widower of about 4 months and she a widow some six weeks." Some women clearly spelled out their intentions and requirements. One newspaper advertisement read:

A Husband Wanted

"By a lady who can wash, cook, scour, sew, milk, spin, weave, hoe (can't plow), cut wood, make fires, feed the pigs, raise chickens, rock the cradle (gold rocker, I thank you, Sir!), saw a plank, drive nails, etc. These are a few of the solid branches; now for the ornamental. 'Long time age' she went as far as syntax, read Murray's Geography and through two rules in Pike's Grammar. Could find 6 states on the Atlas, could read, and you see she can write. Can—no could—paint roses, butterflies, ships &c, but now she can paint houses, whitewash fences, &c.

Now for her terms. Her age is none of your business. She is neither handsome nor a fright, yet an *old* man need *not* apply, nor any who have not a little more education than she has, and a great deal more gold, for there must be $20,000 settled on her before she will bind herself to perform all the above."

Coming to California provided freedom and a new start for people. In 1855 Mary Jane Megquier wrote: "The very air I breathe seems so very free that I have not the least desire to return [to Maine]." One illiterate Missouri emigrant was so pleased with his success in California that he bought a fine suit of clothes. Since he looked so smart, he decided to become a doctor. Another man was surprised and asked him what he knew about practicing medicine. The man said, "Well, not much; but I get all I can do, and I kill just as few as any of them."

In the late 1840s, San Francisco was nearly abandoned by people leaving for the goldfields. During the 1850s, though, the city was an exciting place to be. The economy was strong with gold coming from the mountains. There was an average of thirty new houses built each day, plus two murders and one fire. Prices were high and gambling halls brought in hundreds of thousands of dollars in gold each day. The streets were rumored to be paved with gold, but they weren't paved at all. In the rainy season, or even at high tide, people had to jump from board to board to avoid the mud in the streets. Ships came from around the world, bringing miners. Often, the crew decided to become miners also. They abandoned the ships, leaving them to rot in the harbor. Some ships were run aground and leased as stores and hotels. Fires were frequent. San Francisco burned six times in eighteen months with losses of $25 million and hundreds of lives. Wooden buildings burned quickly and even a supposedly fireproof iron building literally melted. The city came back bigger and better after each fire. Swampy land around the bay was filled to make more land for building.

San Francisco was the place the miners went to spend some of their gold on entertainment. From 1848 until the mid-1850s when the boom slowed, $345 million dollars arrived in the city. Some was spent on solid investments and some on wild celebrations. The miners would usually rent a hotel room, get a shave and haircut, enjoy a restaurant meal, and find entertainment in a gambling hall. Some miners even considered it bad luck to head back to the mines if they had not spent every ounce of gold they had brought with them!

   GA1502

Making a Fortune as a Merchant–Inventing Levi's
Life in California During the Gold Rush

Mining for gold made some people rich, but many barely broke even because of the high cost of goods. It was the merchants and developers who generally made the most money. They provided the equipment, transportation, food, supplies, and entertainment for the miners. "Mining the miners" was the real California bonanza!

One of these merchants who made a fortune was Levi Strauss. At age 17, Strauss had come to the United States from Germany in 1847. He became a draper (cloth seller) in Louisville, Kentucky, but decided to follow the gold rush. To earn money for land and supplies in California, he took a few bolts of cloth on the ship when he sailed from New York in 1850. By the time he reached San Francisco, he had sold everything except some canvas tenting. He hoped to sell it for tents or wagon covers. However, the miners found their clothes wore out quickly from the rough work among the rocks and water. Strauss made some canvas trousers to sell to the miners. More and more miners came to Strauss to buy his "Levi's." He soon forgot about his own mining and started a business selling pants. Levi's were also bought by railroad workers and cowboys. He wrote to his brothers in Kentucky to send more canvas.

Strauss and his partner, Jake Davis, patented the use of little copper rivets to reinforce the seams of his pants. Prospector Alkali Ike had the habit of stuffing his pants pockets so full of ore samples that the pockets ripped open. Ike often took his Levi's to his tailor, Jake Davis, to have them resewn. After several attempts to fix them, Davis took Ike's torn pants to the local blacksmith and had him put rivets at the pocket corners. It worked! Ike's pockets stopped tearing and rivets were then added to other pants. In 1937 the rivets on the back pockets were replaced by heavy stitching when teachers complained they scratched school furniture.

Strauss dedicated himself to continually improving his pants. He bought an even stronger cloth that was produced mainly in the town of Nimes (pronounced neem), France. The French called the material serge de Nimes–meaning cloth from Nimes. By the time it reached America, people just called it "denim." He also decided to dye the material a dark indigo blue which gave a more consistent dye color. These improved pants sold for $13.50 a dozen. "Jeans" was an American pronunciation of Genoa, a town in Italy that also produced this fabric. By the end of the nineteenth century, his plant in San Francisco employed five hundred workers. He made about a million dollars a year and became famous for his Levi's, which are still popular today.

Making a Fortune as a Merchant–Inventing Levi's Activity

Invent something that would have helped the California gold rush miners. This should be a "fantasy" and not exist today.

1. Draw a poster to show your invention. This should be similar to the one for "Fastening Pocket-Openings." On your poster, and in the same locations as on the real poster, put your name, invention name, a patent number, patent date, drawing, a place for witnesses to sign, and the signature of the inventor.

2. On the back of the poster, write a detailed description of your invention, telling what "need" it fulfills and how it works.

3. You might want to research other merchants who became rich during the California gold rush, such as Collis Huntington, Mark Hopkins, Charles Crocker, Philip Armour, John Studebaker, and Leland Stanford.

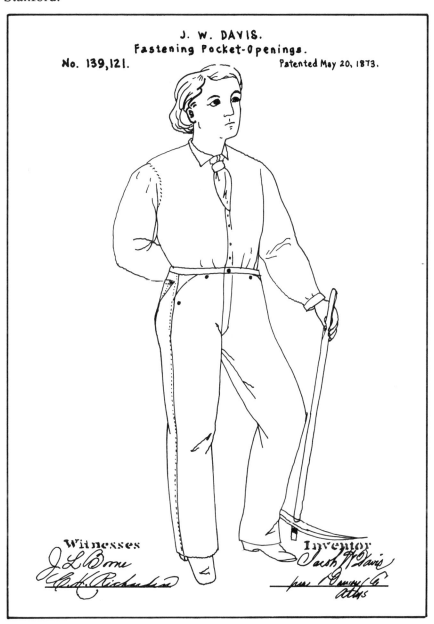

Bibliography

Books

The California Trail by George R. Stewart. Lincoln, NE: University of Nebraska Press, 1962. Very detailed description of the California Trail emigration. Information is organized by years of travel from 1841-1859.

The California Trail Yesterday & Today–A Pictorial Journey Along the California Trail by William E. Hill. Boulder, CO: Pruett Publishing Company, 1986. History of the California Trail, maps, journal quotes, guidebooks, plus early sketches of sites with comparisons to present-day photographs.

Emigrant Trails West by Devere and Helen Helfrich and Thomas Hunt. Klamath Falls, OR: Craft Printers, Inc., 1984. Guide for driving the California, Applegate, Lassen, and Nobles' emigrant trails in Idaho, Nevada, and California. Each trail location is described through emigrant journals, with photographs and a complete map section.

Ghost Trails to California by Thomas H. Hunt. Palo Alto, CA: American West Publishing Company, 1974. Classic California Trail book giving background information on the emigrants, Indians, the land, and the trail. Nine parts of the trail are photographed and explained in detail. Biographical sketches and many detailed maps are included.

Gold Dust by Donald Dale Jackson. Lincoln, NE: University of Nebraska Press, 1980. Extremely detailed book that tells the story of the California Gold Rush, including maps and Forty-Niner portraits.

Nevada's Black Rock Desert by Sessions S. Wheeler. Caldwell, ID: Caxton Printers, Ltd., 1985. Information on the desert itself, Indians, emigrant routes, mining, and ranching in Nevada's Black Rock Desert.

Pathways of America: The Oregon Trail by Lynda Hatch. Carthage, IL: Good Apple, 1994. Detailed accurate historical information, resources, bibliography, and activities on the Oregon Trail for teachers, students, and families. Since much of the California Trail followed the Oregon Trail, this book will help the California Trail teacher, as well.

The Pioneers by the editors of Time-Life Books. Alexandria, VA: Time-Life Books, Inc., 1974. As part of the Old West Series, this book describes the various westward emigrations. Contains Western paintings, sketches, and early photographs.

Prairie Schooner Detours by Irene D. Paden. St. Louis, MO: The Patrice Press, 1990–originally printed by Macmillan in 1949, the centennial year of the Gold Rush. Descriptions of two "shortcuts" traveled by emigrants to California, the Lassen Cutoff and Hastings Cutoff. The book took the author fifteen years to write since she thoroughly explored the routes and read all available journals.

They Saw the Elephant–Women in the California Gold Rush by Jo Ann Levy. Hamden, CT: The Shoe String Press, 1990. Stories of how women experienced their travels to California across the plains, across the Isthmus of Panama, and on ships around Cape Horn. The book also covers the lives of the women once they reached California.

Trails West by Special Publications Division. Washington, DC: National Geographic Society, 1979. Information and photographs on these trails West: Oregon, Santa Fe, Mormon, California, Gila, and Bozeman.

Wagons West Trail Tales 1848 by Robert Shellenberger. Stockton, CA: Heritage West Books, 1991. Collection of California Trail emigrant stories from 1848 which started as a series of articles for a historical society and was compiled into the book.

Wagon Wheel Kitchens by Jacqueline Williams. Lawrence, KS: University Press of Kansas, 1993. Descriptions of emigrant meals on the Oregon Trails including available food, cooking procedures, equipment, festivities, plus extensive journal quotes.

Women's Diaries of the Westward Journey by Lillian Schlissel. New York: Schocken Books, 1982. Information of families on the trails from 1841-50, 1851-55, and 1856-67, plus emigrant diaries of four women: Lydia A. Rudd, Amelia S. Knight, Catherine Haun, and Jane G. Tourtillott.

Other Sources for Studying the California Trail

Oregon-California Trails Association, P.O. Box 1019, Independence, MO 64051-0519, Phone and FAX (812) 252-2276. This large national organization includes the quarterly publication of the *Overland Journal*, regional newsletters, national and local conventions, tours, and trail preservation. OCTA has a catalog available for maps, trail merchandise, books, back issues of the journal, and a special section for children.

Gold Rush–A Simulation of Life and Adventure in a Frontier Mining Camp by Myron Flindt. Lakeside, CA: Interact Company, 1978. This company publishes many simulations that stress cooperative learning and problem solving. Students learn of the excitement and challenges of a nineteenth-century gold rush. As members of mining teams, students must overcome obstacles such as disease, lack of food, harsh weather, and crime as they search for gold. While learning about gold mining, they also improve listening skills, outlining, note-taking, and write a brief research report. A catalog is available from Interact, P.O. Box 997-Y89, Lakeside, CA 92040, Phone: (619) 448-1474.

Every effort has been made, at the time of publication, to insure the accuracy of the information included in this book. We cannot guarantee, however, that the agencies and organizations we have mentioned will continue to operate or to maintain these current locations indefinitely.